FEMALE SEXUAL AROUSAL & THE PINK PILL

Undisclosed Truths About Female Sexual Arousal, What Men Can Do & Whether the FDA Should Have Approved The Pink Pill, Flibanserin (Addyi®)

CAXTON OPERE, MD

Female Sexual Arousal
&
The Pink Pill

Published by Divorce Prevention Inc., a Division of KOTH CLINIC, Inc. Frisco, Texas

FEMALE SEXUAL AROUSAL & THE PINK PILL-Undisclosed Truths About Female Sexual Arousal, What Husbands Can Do & Whether the FDA Should Have Approved The Pink Pill, Flibanserin (Addyi®)

© 2015 by Caxton Opere
ISBN 978-0-9703119-6-2

Unless otherwise indicated, all scripture quotations are from the Holy Bible, Authorized King James Version (KJV)

Disclaimer

The reader acknowledges that the author and publisher are not liable for any choices the reader makes using the information in this book. The reader by purchasing this book agrees not to hold the publisher or author liable for any decisions made based on the information in the book. If you need help choosing a mate, providing or obtaining premarital counseling or handling problems in your relationship you should get professional help.

All characters mentioned in the book are fictitious.

TABLE OF CONTENTS

Acknowledgements
Preface
Introduction

ACKNOWLEDGEMENTS

A man can only have the guts to write a book such as this if he has one hundred percent support from his wife. So naturally, I want to give honor to my lovely ever passionate and supportive darling wife, Id. Hard to find a love like yours, even twenty years ago. Our love is the reason this book and its contents will be celebrated around the world. Your love inspires and challenges me to be better and to never be afraid of the differences between the sexes. You've taught me that the difference between the sexes can be celebrated and should not become the battle between the sexes.

I am thankful to God, for designing sex between a husband and wife as the most legitimate and intoxicating of all pleasures.

Lastly but not least, I wish to thank you the reader for summoning the courage to pick up and read this book. Never look back. Hopefully, you'll use what you learn and become better in your relationships and in helping others find the life-giving hidden source of joy that comes through healthy intimacy.

PREFACE

Sex is a marriage lifeline, pleasurable and sweet. It soothes the pains, heals the psyche and drives our innermost passions. It can effortless do the work of a magnet, dynamo, battery, generator, doctor, nurse, surgeon, psychiatrist, father, mother and best friend all combined. It is more effective as an elixir than antibiotics, antidepressants, vitamins and psychotherapy in instilling the will to live. In a marriage, sex can say without words those deepest of yearnings words can never do justice to. It elevates, motivates, comforts, relaxes and accentuates life. It gives meaning and freshness to the meaning of love in marriage. Sex in marriage unites two souls in a most gentle yet gushingly inexplicable empowering but not overpowering way that reflects a divine gift of immeasurable pleasure and kindness. Life is released through sex and celebrated through it. Sex creates an atmosphere between those who regularly enjoy its benefits in a marriage that cannot be traded for anything else. Sex is the one thing for which any married couple cannot afford to have a surrogate. For men, sex is the number one item on their marriage priority. It is not so for wives.

God wants husbands and wives to perfectly blend sexually and to have a taste of heaven through sexual intimacy.

> *Therefore shall a man leave his father and his mother, and shall cleave unto his wife: and they shall be one flesh. And they were both naked, the man and his wife, and were not ashamed. Genesis 2:24-45*

While I stand to be corrected, I still think God put a little piece of heaven in our wives! As a result of what God put in them, women are more erotic, exotic, colorful, sexually interesting, more sexually attractive and more sexually responsive to different sexual stimuli. No woman can run away from this erotic part of her self, even though some, particularly Christian women some of whom I have counseled in the past, try very hard to run away from their erotic nature. Some become unavailable, asexual or heterophobic. I coined the word heterophobic to mean someone who hates the union between a male man and a female woman! Trying very hard to suppress their erotic self, a woman may bury herself in her business, office work, housework, church work, religion, busy schedule, childcare or household chores. Personally, it's now an annoying cliché to read about the busy wife who comes home from work complaining of having so much to do all day she has no time for intimate moments with the person she now considers an inconsiderate immature husband. Most such women will end up alone or on antidepressants. Such marriages eventually end in shambles except the woman and not the man does something different or even drastic. Yet Dr. Chivers in an interview with Daniel Bergner bestselling author of *What Do Women Want*, says it is the woman who chooses this behavior of sexual distancing because she is sure her husband is trapped in the marriage.

While some deny their erotic self, others have a distorted view of sex and their sexuality. This latter group consists of men and women who believe that sex is filthy, unnecessary and something to stay away from even after getting married. Most come from religious backgrounds or they have a history of sexual molestation or distorted indoctrination. To enjoy the natural gift of sex in your marriage, you must delete from your mind the idea that sex is dirty, filthy or the 'forbidden fruit' that Eve gave to Adam. Sexual organs did not grow on Adam and Eve by some strange mutation after they ate of the forbidden fruit. Both had their organs intact before eating of the tree of knowledge of good and evil. We all know that women naturally want to give yet when it comes to sexual intimacy in marriage, wives give far less than they promised their husbands. Is there something we're missing in the marriage dynamics that makes a wife give less and less sexually in their marriages as the years go by, even in non-abusive healthy marriages?

Despite the woman's desire for romance and sexual intimacy, we men often fail to understand our wives or enjoy that piece of heaven God gave them. And for this, we often pay a heavy price. Women need to be played with, laughed with, cared for and sometimes cried with so they can always have a piece of "heaven" for us husbands. If as husbands we do any less, she might have an affair with herself, her work, her busy schedule or career or her narcissistic world in which she is queen and her husband a slave eunuch. She'll play that role out every night with her husband to the man's detriment–a eunuch after all needs no sex! The job of a husband is to become his wife's secret lover, a wild yet caring, compassionate caveman. If you understand that the female brain is far more active

8

in many different areas than the man's, you'll carefully follow the Bible's recommendations to dwell with the wife according to knowledge, specialized knowledge of what arouses your wife. If men would do that, provided the woman is not denying her erotic self or trying to be asexual, he'll have a different wife by "Friday". For those men who have been enjoying the best their wives have to offer, why stop now? Keep doing all the good things you've been doing to keep you and your wife happy. Isn't it safer to cry with her than to cry alone in the doghouse? Or isn't it better to laugh with her instead of becoming the laughing stock of your friends after the alimony settlements? Isn't it easier to learn to love and cherish her rather than learn to live with regret when she's gone? Isn't it easier to learn to live a rich life together than to live on what's left after your paycheck is split by the divorce courts? It is.

Sex is the mind's greatest stimulant and remains the most pleasurable experience to have this side of eternity. Just the mere thought of sex can bring some women to orgasms. Daniel G Amen, bestselling author and psychiatrist said the brain is the largest sex organ, so use it wisely. Sex is God's gift of pleasure and we must learn how to handle it in its safest and most rewarding environment, in marriage.

We haven't properly addressed female sexual arousal or the erotic nature of our women in the boardroom, bedroom, pulpit, or physician's office. At least not in ways that would help our women feel understood and loved and our men more skilled at dealing with their wives and satisfying them sexually. This is quite evident in most Christian marriages. As the world's leading expert on the medical complications of divorce, a husband, an internist, Marriage Building Expert^{SM}, a pastor for over eleven years who has developed a marriage building framework and won Tumblr's 2015 award for *100 Hottest Non-Profit Startups* for my work on *The Divorce Medicine Project*, I believe the natural rhythms behind female sexual arousal, the very things that bond women to their husbands with greater deeper loving connections, has already been disrupted by unnatural work schedules, the lies of militant feminism, increasing anti-God behavior, pornography and economic instability. We need to restore sanity and dignity, deeper intimacy in our homes through the messages we share about female sexuality.

This book is written for four main reasons. First is to help everyone interested in sexual intimacy, female sexual arousal, how it differs from male sexual arousal and how a multiple number of factors play a role in determining female sexual arousal and desire. Only a sound knowledge of these things will get a woman aroused and enjoy intimacy on a healthy and frequent basis without using a drug with questionable efficacy and serious side effects. The second reason is to help Pink prescribers and potential users understand and interpret the seemingly complex clinical trial data that led to the FDA approval of flibanserin. You'll be able to draw your own conclusions about the effectiveness of Pink and whether to prescribe or take the drug. The third reason is to outline both the reported and predictable adverse effects of flibanserin for both prescribers and the women who want to take the pill. The fourth reason is to help couples build a loving sexually fulfilling marriage through a clearer knowledge of the factors that turn both partners on or off. The fifth one is to encourage couples to lay aside all their superfluity of naughtiness and other common excuses like migraine headaches that eventually wear down their marriage and break up their homes through sexual starvation. As with every writer, I have this hope that the book will deliver many marriages from the dungeons of sexual starvation, deprivation and ignorance and the marital collapse that inevitably follows such sickened marriages. I also hope that our wives would cease from suppressing their erotic selves, become more seductive and inflame a passion in their men that would cause those men to continually woo and lovingly satisfy their wives' deepest cravings in the marriage for decades to come. Provided of course that these men are being rewarded bountifully in the bedroom!

Caxton Opere, MD
Frisco, TX. October 2015

INTRODUCTION

Everything we love about heterosexual marital sex is intimately tied to our fascination about female sexuality. Simply stated, women are not just beautiful, they are intriguing in a fascinating, alluring, mysterious and never ending seductive erotic way that no one can ever explain. Even straight women find women attractive and capable of arousing sexual feelings in them. Every part of a woman's body, perhaps with the exception of her ears, can arouse a man sexually to a point where he is willing to drop everything and lose anything just to be with her. We can deny this but it won't change the facts. Thrones, presidencies, corporate headships, professorships have all been won and lost because of this allure of the woman. Such power! Intriguing and will always be. When interviewing the late British Nobel Laureate Doris Lessing on *Psychology Today*'s December 12, 2013 online issue, Dr. Robert J King's article ended with the irrefutable conclusion that women are a lot more interesting sexually than men. I don't think this conclusion will be up for debate any time soon.

This book is divided into three main sections. The first section, AROUSAL, addresses female sexual arousal. The second PINK PILL addresses clinical trial findings, issues of validity, efficacy, side effects and the future predicted adverse effects based on pharmacology. The third section deals with RELATIONSHIPS and sexual intimacy in marriage. There will be some overlap but these are the main sections. There is also an appendix The words flibanserin, Pink, pink pill and Addyi will be used interchangeably throughout the book. So come along on this fantastic voyage into the land of seduction, statistics, clinical trials and the feminine mystique.

PART 1
AROUSAL

Chapter 1

SEX-STARVED?

It's now been several years since I wrote a letter of suspension to a female church member for refusing to canoodle with her devoted husband. The issue had come to my attention on a warm Saturday afternoon over a decade ago. I was at a meeting when I received a distress phone call from someone that the woman's husband had threatened to burn down his own house. Rushing over to the couple's house, I met a lady at the door who told me that both husband and wife were inside the house, and left hurriedly. I walked in to the house of this God-fearing couple and found no flame-throwers, propellant, smoke and most importantly, no evidence that the man had lost his mind. I left the house and simply took the husband with me. It turned out the man was about to burn down his own house in frustration because his wife deprived him consistently and insanely of bedroom privileges and that day was his birthday. He was dying on the inside because his sexual needs were completely neglected and he wanted to go out in a dignified way. He was one of several that I have ministered to or listened to over the last twenty years. This seemed to be the most life-threatening case I've ever seen but I'm sure there are more out there.

A few years earlier in 1996, an upset female pastor in Washington DC called me about a difficult marital situation involving one of the deacons in her church. She informed me that this well-rounded, good husband and father of three kids had told his wife that he was going to go out and cheat on her. The preacher was upset with the man because she felt he wasn't making any sense. Why would he, a church deacon even think of doing such a foolish thing, she had added? It sounded strange that the man was warning his wife before hand. It seemed the man wasn't getting Steve Harvey's "cookies" in bed. So I told her that if a man tells his wife he is going to cheat on her without actually having done so, it means he is warning her to stop doing something bad that could lead him to cheating. That was when the lady pastor said the man had complained that his wife had sex with him only once a year. I won't be surprised if the wife were present and argued that the man forgot he got something extra on their honeymoon! They had been married for three years and he had sex only thrice. The man got something after they married and once every year thereafter.

> Janice is a 39-year old lady with a degree in theology on the East Coast. She met my wife after she had developed some of the medical complications of marital stress outlined in my book *Divorce Medicine*. She complained day and night about her "evil" stingy husband whenever she spoke about him. One day she saw the way my wife and I played with each other without seeing

how we fought, and immediately felt comfortable about sharing her concerns with me. Following her typical gripe, I gave her a simple assignment. She should write down thirty things she hated most about her husband and five excellent qualities about him. The reason for the latter excellent qualities was because I suspected she didn't like anything about her husband as a result of her own doing. Six months went by without her producing anything positive while she kept her negative grind. One night I asked my wife to write down two questions she must ask her the very next day and insist on answers. The first question was when last did she sleep with her husband. The second question was how often per year in the last twenty years of their marriage had she slept with the man. To the first the lady said eight months ago, and to the second she said four times a year. These were a young able-bodied couple.

Do you know any young man that marries and wants to sleep with his wife only twice a year? Not unless he has other problems.

Juanita is a pretty young Mexican lady living in California and married to a devoted husband and gentleman. They have no children. Her husband complained that sex once every five or six weeks is creating problems for him. He saw a urologist who recommended more frequent intercourse. He doted over his wife and the wife agreed that she couldn't imagine finding another more devoted husband if she lost this one. Yet every night at bedtime, she would take a shower, stimulate her husband's mind and give the impression that it was going to be an awesome night. But rather than come to bed, she would go to the laundry room and start doing laundry way past midnight. This has been going on for over a decade.

The reason for the sex-starvation experienced by the men in these stories may be due to female sexual interest/arousal disorder (FSIAD) or sexual indifference. If FSIAD is due to a psychiatric or psychological problem, flibanserin may very well provide a solution. Will it? About 10 percent of women have female sexual interest/arousal disorder and the pink pill might be helpful. So I have great hopes that drugs like flibanserin would address these challenging situations in these and other sex-starved marriages and restore love passion and fulfillment. Regardless of my hopes however, the possibilities of what the pink pill can do based on the clinical trials reported by the FDA are not very encouraging.

Chapter 2

SEXUAL AVAILABILITY RULES

The following rules can help you and your spouse boost sexual intimacy instantly, particularly if you already understand each other's *5 Love Languages®*. Follow these rules of sexual availability everyday.

FOR THE WOMAN
RULE #1: Just because you don't feel like you're ready doesn't mean you're not ready.

Studies are showing that a woman can be sexually aroused as measured by lab instruments while she denies such arousal. Objective measurements can confirm arousal but subjectively, the woman may still deny that she is aroused. It's as if the woman is dissociating herself from what's going on in her own body. If kept going however, such dissonance could lead to disruption of healthy sexual activity and the marriage itself. Women need to therefore be comfortable with their own body when it suggests arousal particularly in their own marriages with their own husbands. Women do not routinely have spontaneous arousal like men when exposed to sexual stimuli. Instead, they have a more refined form of sexual arousal called reactive arousal. Reactive arousal means she decides if she wants to respond to the sexual stimulus and choose whether or not to engage in the activity. Even if the sexual stimulus leads to arousal, she may not develop a desire until certain other conditions are met. Money, an apology, a promise not to invite the mother in-law for Christmas, a credit card, chocolates, gifts or simple acts of kindness are examples of the conditions a husband may have to agree to. Even if she will enjoy the act, a woman can still claim she is not aroused when those physiological changes suggest she is. Many women supposing that they should experience spontaneous arousal like men as portrayed deceptively by the media, have destroyed the love and tenderness their husbands had towards them by ignoring his needs. Don't ignore your husband's needs as your needs may be met while you're meeting his. Be available for your husband. Refusing to meet a husband's needs creates a hostile environment that becomes toxic to the well being of both partners. If that's what the woman wants she'll get plenty of it until they both destroy the marriage.

FOR THE MAN
RULE #2: Always remember that your second time around is always better for the wife.

Your first orgasm is often for you as a man. The woman is rarely ready for an orgasm when you are except you've mastered the art of preparing her through seduction and foreplay. So unless your performance is limited by health reasons, you should always prepare for a second "round" to meet your wife's own orgasmic needs. This is usually between five to thirty minutes after your own first orgasm. A woman peaks to orgasm much more slowly and satisfying that need guarantees that next time, you'll get the favor returned. Women don't forget such things easily and her memory of what happened the last time you were together in bed is itself a female aphrodisiac. Less excited after the first orgasm, you're more likely to hold on longer for her to reach orgasm before you have your second one. If you can't hold because you're excited, then go on to your third leg. Changing positions may also significantly help both of you reach orgasm. Be available for your wife even if that means getting Viagra®.

FOR BOTH HUSBAND AND WIFE
RULE #3:
Understand what turns a woman on and give her that.

Women like agile athletic strong men, so get in shape. Don't think that because you've married her you don't have to maintain your physical body. You do. Smell your armpits and your clothes particularly those parts where your arms suck up your clothes. If you don't like what you smell, what makes you think your wife will? Run your finger through the inside of your thigh in the space between your thigh and scrotum and smell it. Yes, smell it. If you don't like the smell, how dare you try to get in bed with your wife with those two areas stinking? She's someone's daughter for crying out loud! Take a shower. Some men pride themselves on the Afro they have been nursing in their armpits since high school. Clip the hair or even better ask your wife what she wants you to do with it. Don't be shocked if she says "I'm glad you finally asked". Do you have real bad breath and need to see a dentist for a cavity? Then gargle with peroxide at least once every three to four days and use regular mouthwash more frequently. Brush your teeth daily and at night before going to bed. Start learning to approach your wife with freshness and some cologne smelling on you as if you're going out on a date. She just might ask you out and give you a night to remember. Wash your clothes and dry them in the hot sun whenever you can so they can have a real freshness to them. The sun's UV light destroys far more bacteria than the heat from the dryer. I don't use the dryer for my underwear and regularly dry my clothes in the sun. For women, a nice fresh smell can be an aphrodisiac according to University of Texas at Austin Psychology Professors Cindy Meston and David Buss. When a husband and wife feel a sense of duty towards meeting each other's needs and this feeling is reciprocated, the marriage is likely to enjoy the benefits of greater physical intimacy.

SEXUAL INCONTINENCY
Incontinence is an inability to hold an urge or desire. Incontinence may be for emotions, words, urine, feces or sex. Once a man gets married, a mental gate is opened in his mind that makes it easier to arouse him sexually far more than when he was single. He becomes sexually incontinent and therefore more vulnerable to sexual temptation. It may also be that his natural preservative instinct guards that gate carefully until he marries. Either way you look at it, once he marries, the gate is now wide open. Carefully

guarding the gate becomes an important task for every man after marriage whether or not he is exposed to temptation.

For men physical intimacy equals emotional intimacy. They feel a woman has responded to them emotionally if they can be physically intimate with her. For women the reverse is often the case. Emotional intimacy must always precede physical intimacy. This rule holds except for nymphomaniacs and rape when all the rules get thrown out the window and there is always a price to pay for breaking the rules. If you want your husband to connect with you emotionally connect with him sexually. Similarly for the man, if you want your wife to connect with you sexually, connect with her emotionally.

THE COOLIDGE EFFECT
In farm animals, the male tends to seek out variety in its choice of females to mate with. Some male animals will never mate with a female twice. Even when attempts are made by the farmer to disguise the female with odors or blindfolding the male, it may not work. The story was narrated about a day President Coolidge and his wife visited a government farm in Kentucky. On arrival, the President was separated from his wife and both were given separate guided tours. On arrival at the poultry, Mrs. Coolidge asked the guide how often the rooster would perform its male role on the hens. Dozens of times, the guide replied. "Tell that to the President", Mrs. Coolidge replied. When the message got to President Coolidge, he was dumbfounded. So after musing about what to say,

he asked the guide, if the dozens of mounts was with one female. The tour guide replied, that it was with a different female each time. Tell that to Mrs. Coolidge, President Coolidge responded. The summary of this is that highly civilized men learn to curtail their Coolidge tendencies. The other side of the Coolidge effect quantified by Beamer, Bermant and Clegg (1960) shows how the male sheep takes increasingly more time just to reach orgasm when presented with the same female during the mating period. When the same ram was presented with five different females at different mating times, it took the ram under 2 minutes to complete the act with each female. When the ram was given the same female sheep at five different times, the period to ejaculation increased to almost 18 minutes.

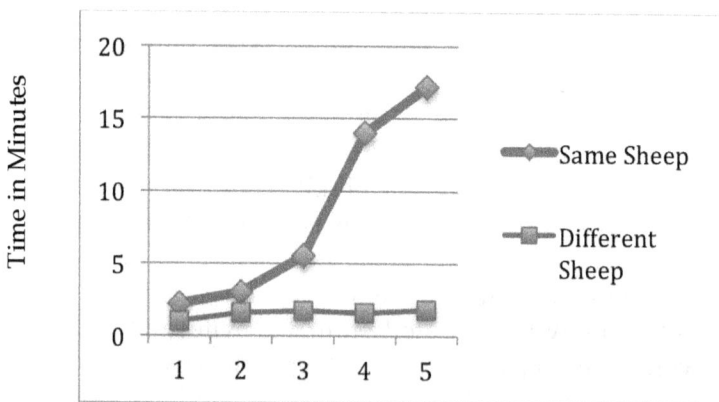

Figure 1. Difference between having one or multiple mating partners for one ram. Source: *Beamer, Bermant & Clegg, 1960.*

How does this Coolidge effect apply to humans? First the more excited your man is about you, the less time he'll take to reach an orgasm. So if your man reaches orgasm in about 2 minutes, it's either because he is tired, too excited or sex-starved. Be patient and remind him of rule #2 above. The male reaches orgasm before the female naturally. Give him about 5 minutes recovery time. If you're frustrated and never reach an orgasm while he reaches his in two minutes, it may be because you're both impatient. Even though he has reached orgasm, you are just building up the tempo. Let your husband know that. Invite him back to bed, talk to each other and give each other a massage. If your husband has been sex-starved it will take time to feed him and nourish him sexually to that point where his only desire is to please you in bed. If you push him away because he had his own orgasm before yours, you're pushing nature away and you may not like the consequences. Secondly, without God or the law, most men will philander at the drop of a hat. However if he stays with one woman and learns to love her and is able to bring her to orgasm, meaning he spends eighteen minutes or more in the act, something different takes place in the relationship. They experience a deeper intimate connection, what the Bible calls knowing each other. This knowledge is one of deepened intimacy spirit soul and body between husband and wife. This deepening intimacy, if nurtured by continued kindness towards each other in a normal healthy relationship outside the bedroom, will lead to continuous excitement decades after marriage that philanderers cannot ever understand. The philanderer ram is usually finished in less than two minutes each time a different female is introduced.

Chapter 3

FEMININE FANTASTIC

THE FEMALE BODY AND FEMALE AROUSAL

The female nude body is the most mysterious, enthralling, alluring, adored and exciting object in all of creation. Nothing created by God or man on this planet can be so breathtaking as this object of every man's sexual fantasy. No car, house or man-made structure can take the place of the allure of beautiful women naked or not. Even straight women are excited and aroused by looking at a naked woman's body in motion according to Dr. Meredith Chivers' multiple studies on the subject reported in the 2007 volume 93 issue 6 of the *Journal of Personality and Social Psychology*. I must warn that most of Dr. Chivers' studies on the subject of female sexual arousal are not for the faint at heart, spiritually immature, sexually deprived or those at risk of engaging in pornography. The latter include those who have been sexually starved in a monogamous relationships, particularly Christian men. A woman arouses embers of passion in both sexes just by her being a woman. A woman rarely has a problem inspiring feelings of lust and sexual desire in the opposite sex. Men desire women. They were designed and wired from the Garden of

Eden for just that. If they don't desire the woman, naked or not, that man immediately recognizes there is a problem, whether it be sexual orientation or erectile dysfunction. So a woman creating sexual arousal in others has rarely been the problem. As a matter of fact when getting aroused became a problem, curbing the problem became a number one priority and both prostitution and the pornography industry were born. When a man could not get it up, it was immediately called impotence and later erectile dysfunction, (ED). Scientists worked in a frenzy day and night to find a cure. Different gadgets and eventually pills culminating in the blockbuster pill Viagra emerged. Today, pornography is a $12 billion industry and sales of Viagra rake in $2 billion dollars annually.

A man must be able to enjoy sex with his wife. If he can't, he usually admits he has a problem and tries to solve the problem. He takes ownership of the problem because he was designed to enjoy this greatest of pleasures and knows he is missing out on something great. Napoleon Hill called sex the mind's greatest stimulant, capable of bestowing superhuman powers on men. It is far more motivating than any intoxicant drug you can think of. Used aright, this innate desire for sex in a man can raise him to the greatest heights of accomplishment and creativity or sink him to the lowest pit and station in life. Perverted outside of its original purpose, it becomes destructive, as measured by the negative effects of adultery, pornography, sexually transmitted diseases, abortion, AIDS, hepatitis, crime rates, prostitution and the violence associated with sex-related crimes.

In contrast, when a woman has a problem enjoying sexual intimacy in her marriage, she may feel fine. She may not even feel there is a problem, until a crisis develops related to her lack of desire, arousal or availability to her husband. Then what happens next? Would it be marriage counseling, infidelity, divorce or Pink? The woman decides which it would be. If effective, flibanserin may have brought in a fourth option for the married woman with low sexual desire. Can Pink really save sex-starved marriage or reduce the likelihood of divorce in such a marriage? What if a woman becomes divorced while on Pink and decides to stop the drug? Can she stop taking Pink right away or does she need to taper the dose gradually? Are poor responders to the pink pill less likely or more likely to develop complications from withdrawal? Is there any clinical trial indicating that a withdrawal discontinuation syndrome will not occur?

So why design a pill for women, the pink pill, flibanserin, trade name Addyi? With all the desire and talk about sex, why would anyone think that women still need a pill for improving their arousal? Is the arousal pill for lesbian women or just for heterosexual women? What type of women would benefit the most from using Pink? FSIAD obviously has different causes and while the clinical trials lumped all the women together, it has diminished the study impact on the sub-type in which it would be most effective. As a minister and physician evaluating couples over more than two decades and learning about the problems, I have observed and suspect a sub-classification of FSIAD. Not all women with FSIAD or HSDD are the same. While the clinical trials lumped them all together, you will see by the time you finish this book, why such lumping may very well be sexist and ineffective in helping address the FSIAD epidemic. That may be where DSM-V has failed women in its criteria for female sexual interest/arousal disorder. All women with FSIAD or HSDD are not the same and cannot be treated the same way.

WOMEN vs. MEN, SEXUALLY SPEAKING

Women that take good care of their minds and bodies can be sexually attractive or "hot" but their hotness doesn't translate into instant readiness for sex. Men are always ready. Women are not easily aroused sexually. Men are! Women do not follow a linear Pavlov stimulus-response curve when it comes to sexual desire. Men do. All these in-built female responses help preserve the dignity, health, freedom and wellbeing of our women. This will in turn protect and improve the overall conditions of our society at large. Imagine what could happen if simple sexual stimuli triggered sexual desires in women as it usually does in men. By the time a sexually active woman reaches menopause, she may have had 15 to 30 pregnancies. With one pregnancy roughly every nine months and then nursing the baby for at least another six months, many women will spend the most productive years of their life just getting pregnant! Let's assume an average woman starts having babies at age nineteen. Twenty pregnancies carried for nine months gives 180 months of pregnancy. If each baby is then nursed for another six months, you get a total of 120 months the woman spends nursing her newborn before she gets pregnant again. The total spent getting pregnant and nursing would be 300 months or twenty-five years. And that means she'll be forty-four by the time she's done with babies. Not good for a country's development or the feminist movement! The hormonal chaos would equally be terrible. The woman will suffer more complications during pregnancy and malnutrition, increased likelihood of complications during the pregnancy. So thank God that most women are not sexually aroused in a simple linear fashion like men! Women, unlike men are sexually aroused in a non-linear fashion. But whoever thought they did?

Studies done by Masters and Johnson in the late sixties through the early seventies gave us a better understanding of sexual arousal and performance phases. They advanced our knowledge of the intimate relationships between men and women scientifically and showed that sexual intercourse is normal and healthy, just like God had told us in the Bible (Genesis 2:24,25; Hebrews 13:4). The book in the Bible that deals almost explicitly with sexual intimacy is the *Songs of Solomon*. Masters and Johnson brought some sense into the act of canoodling for couples that thought there was something dirty and filthy about sex. They however left us with one problem, the idea that men and women are sexually aroused identically in a linear Pavlovian stimulus-response manner. Not only has this deficiency from these world-renowned scientists left the world at the mercy of drug companies trying to design a drug to

30

straighten a woman who fails to respond in the predicted linear fashion like men, they missed the single most important aspect of female sexual arousal, the female brain!

Chapter 4

THE FEMALE BRAIN

According to world-renowned psychiatrist and best selling author, Daniel G. Amen, MD, a woman's brain is significantly different from a man's. It is more active than men's in many areas where men previously thought they had one-up on women such as the prefrontal cortex (PFC). The PFC controls executive functions such as planning and delaying gratification. In addition to having greater activity in the PFC, limbic cortex and hippocampus, women have greater activity in the anterior cingulate cortex of their brains than men. When the anterior cingulate cortex becomes overactive, women become stuck on negative thoughts, unable to shift from those thoughts or move on to something else. These aspects of the female brain cannot be ignored in developing a strategy for addressing the problem of female sexual arousal or the impact of FSIAD on her relationships and overall wellbeing. I believe that women unintentionally ignore the consequences of sexual deprivation on their own health, their husbands and their marriage because of over-activity in their anterior cingulate cortex. Most women we have dealt with in our ministry with sexually deprived husbands are usually fixated on some negative past event. Unfortunately, some of these negative events are unrelated to the husbands they are now punishing. Even if punishing the man is justified initially, such punishment cannot go on indefinitely without ruining her and the marriage. Persistent focus on a negative past enables the negative event to be blown out of proportion and may lead to FSIAD. At that point a woman diagnosed with this subtype of FSIAD needs not just a pill, but psychiatric care. This inability to shift from dominating negative thoughts is probably secondary to pathology involving the anterior cingulate cortex. Identifying this pathology using special brain scans such as PET (photo emission tomography) scans may provide a biological basis for diagnosing the psychiatric condition and treating it. This biological reductionism may be an extreme one, but it should help you see that besides meeting the DSM-V criteria for FSIAD, a few more investigations may be needed before placing a woman on the pink pill.

ANTS in Her Head!

According to Dr. Amen, women are also prone to more ANTs (automatic negative thoughts) about themselves. These negatives must be weighed side-by-side with the special strengths of the woman's brain, five of which Dr. Amen outlined in his book *Unleash The Power of The Female Brain.* These 5 Strengths of the female brain are intuition, empathy, collaboration, self-control and little worry. To gain even greater insight into the female brain, I suggest you see Dr. Jill Bright's TEDx Talk, *My Stroke of Insight.* If a woman balances these five strengths of her brain she will live a long healthy and fulfilling life. Many women however create internal torture for themselves by misusing these strengths. For example, overusing intuition leads to a woman's unnecessary fear and anxiety. Overusing empathy designed for nurturing and caring may lead to doing too much and burn out while overuse of the prefrontal cortex for self-control can morph into her becoming a control freak. There are also some subtle but major differences between the female and male brains that play out in how women perceive sexual encounters. Many of these are highlighted in Dr. Amen's book. The most profound and probably the shortest of these highlights is that women are prone to a kind of perfectionism in which they magnify their flaws and minimize their good points. Too often, they reel their husbands or male partners in into this negative sea and lose far more than is necessary. Sometimes, they both drown in it.

Johnny was up and out of the house on Tuesday election day, about 30 minutes earlier. He had an appointment with some investors that morning and needed to pick up bound presentations at the printer's before the rush hour traffic reached full force. By the time Betty was up, she realized Johnny was gone. Oh I see, she mused. He didn't want to look at me because he thinks I'm now fat and ugly. That's why he kept saying he had so many things on his mind last night. No wonder he has been coming home late (by which she meant 6:15pm instead of 6pm) these past two weeks. He might be cheating on me. But he told me he still loves me. Why would he say he loves me if he thinks I'm fat and ugly? He is a liar. I'll teach him never to lie to me! All this negative chatter was going on in Betty's mind while her husband was trying to secure a multi-million dollar investment. He usually leaves home at 6am but left at 5:30am for the same reason he had been coming home 15 minutes late; meet with investors. By the time Betty had gone through all the negative chatter in her head, she had almost no energy left to get ready for work. Later in the day, she looked up the names of some good divorce lawyers, and prepared for a showdown with Johnny. She arrived home first, got on the scale, saw that she weighed only 109 pounds and had actually lost 3 pounds. Now she was confused about what to do with all the negative chatter bubbling in her head. While frozen on the scale thinking about what to do next and how to justify the ANTs in her head, she heard the garage door opening. She tried to hide the scale and her excitement about her weight loss and instantly felt good about herself. She would let him slide this time, she thought to herself.

The question is what could have happened had Johnny walked in before she could weigh herself? Or what do you think would have happened had she weighed an extra four or five pounds? These are some of the things that may go on in a woman's head and hinder female arousal or sabotage the marriage. These automatic negative thoughts (ANTs) may be eliminated using the four fundamental influencers of thought control. These are Biological, Psychological, Social and Spiritual. The Amen Clinics have integrated these four into a *Four Circles Approach* to create a program for their clients. It is an effective approach and one that cannot be ignored in attempting to address the issue of female sexual arousal. Biology influences your thoughts. Proper rest, nutrition, and avoidance of chemicals such as cocaine that can alter brain function control how you think. How accurately and clearly would you be able to think if you are high on cocaine or some hallucinogen and intoxicated with alcohol? Probably not very clearly! If you're dehydrated, on the verge of experiencing a heat stroke or are about to become comatose from extremely low blood sugars, your thinking is altered. Similarly, if you're angry and upset, prejudiced or racist, chances are high that your interpretation of events will be significantly distorted by your emotions. Unfortunately with charged emotions, your memory and recall may instantly double for your own interpretation of the events. Under those circumstances of charged emotions, you are likely to develop long-term memory of your distorted interpretation of the events. That usually works out poorly for a marriage when a wife then constantly brings up issues she remembers very clearly. One Christian lady once threw out her husband's belongings on their front lawn and threatened to call the police following an argument about finances. The man had no money and no wallet and to avoid police issues left immediately. As he walked down the road, another single lady and member of their church picked him up and put him up for the night. He went back home the next day but a month later, the Good Samaritan single lady informed the man he was pregnant. The man had never cheated on his wife until that night when he became emotionally vulnerable. His wife blamed him constantly for everything that happened and claims she remembered everything that night very clearly. She however conveniently forgot that part where she threatened to call the police and the man had to run out of the house.

No one knows how much of a role ANTS play in female sexual arousal desire disorder but it may be quite significant. Drugs may need to be developed for managing ANTs and perhaps some may already be on the market for other indications.

As you'll see in the next chapter, women do not respond in a simple or linear fashion to sexual cues. Their response is more complex and governed not just by sexual stimuli but biologic and psychological factors. Understanding these different factors as well as the ANTs in the head will help reduce the incidence of FSIAD, make our women happier and more available to their men.

Chapter 5

WHAT AROUSES WOMEN?
Can Men Give It to Them?

What sexually arouses a woman? The answer is not as simple as it is for men. A man can be aroused by as little as a woman's smile, a slit gown and you can fill in the blanks about other single items or cues from a woman that could make any grown man become fully aroused, drop everything and be willing to trade his soul for a brief moment of pleasure! Men can afford to be aroused by anything from a woman after all the eventual and ultimate outcome of intimacy, a pregnancy, is not the man's burden but the woman's!

The idea that women should respond in a linear pattern just like men is absurd if not arrogant. Men and women are not the same and even their brains are different according to psychiatrist Dr. Daniel G. Amen. The presumption that sexual arousal is identical for both men and women has unfortunately lowered some of the expectations husbands have of themselves when it comes to arousing their wives through sensitive intelligent wooing and seduction. The idea that a wife should be wet and ready as soon as she gets in bed with her husband is not only absurd if you know women, it is sexist, untrue to the nature of women and robs the marriage bed of deepening intimacy. It has probably caused the disintegration of many marriages, led to so much pain, frustration, abuse, neglect and divorce. Everyone, including the kids, suffers from this ignorance about what arouses women. It's time for a change.

There are different models used to explain female sexual arousal. In 1966, Masters and Johnson studies described four phases of sexual response: **Excitement/Arousal, Orgasm, Plateau** and **Resolution**. These four included the act itself. Due credit goes to Masters and Johnson for helping us see that these are the key components of sexual arousal and that sexual intimacy is not some filthy trashy shameful thing to be abhorred. They presented sex as a natural healthy and acceptable desire particularly in the context of marriage. Their model however represents what happens in men but not in women. It missed additional elements unique to the female sexual response. In 1979, Kaplan's model described three phases: **Desire, Arousal** and the **Orgasm.** While this model has tried to simplify the sexual response to three simple phases, it excludes the resolution. The resolution phase is an established physiological phase that follows an orgasm during which an orgasm is not possible. So in reality, the Kaplan model is either incomplete or has four phases. Eighteen years later in 1997, Whipple and Brash-McGreer (WBM) described another model with four phases and called it a circular model. The phases are - **Desire/Excitement, Plateau, Orgasm** and **Resolution**. It differs very little from the 1966 version of sexual arousal by Masters and Johnson.

While these three may or may not presume that the woman's sexual response is identical to the man's, in reality it appears so. Rightfully, protests have emerged about all three models as unfitting for women. All three are linear and unidirectional, going from one stage to the next without any possibility of returning to the previous phase once desire is set in motion. As we all know in reality, just because a woman's desire is triggered does not mean she will go along to the next phase and the next. Many men who failed to get this are languishing in jail for attempted date rape.

Figure 2. Sexual Arousal Based on The Masters and Johnson Model.

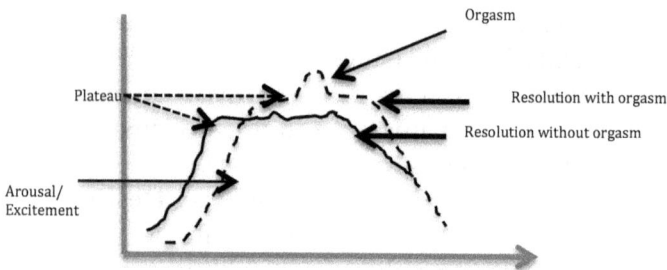

The Masters and Johnson model may belittle the woman's entire femininity and ignore a woman's natural response to sexual encounters; a guarded response to an approaching male. That's why I like some additional features introduced by University of British Columbia's Dr. Rosemary Basson. Dr. Basson's non-linear model of the female sexual response takes into consideration why women behave the way they do sexually in their bedrooms.

In addition to describing a truly circular model, she includes the single most important thing men often miss when seeking bedroom intimacy, the psychological aspect of female sexual arousal. Unlike men, women need more than just a sexual stimulus to be fully aroused and ready. I particularly favor the Basson circular model as it includes the environmental and biological factors influencing the female sexual response. The Basson model provides a more natural and realistic view of how men and women, particularly husbands and wives, interact in real life. The Basson model shows that a sexual stimulus may or may not lead to arousal depending on other psychological and biological factors.

The Reed Model divides the female sexual response into Seduction, Sensation, Surrender and Reflection. The Seduction phase is the desire phase, the period when desire is sparked. The Sensation phase is the phase when arousal is accompanied by the very act of intercourse and leads to excitement and plateauing. The Surrender phase is the orgasm phase and this is followed by the Reflection phase. The Reflection phase is the resolution phase. Shall we continue? Was it good? Do we love each other? All these questions may occur at the reflection phase. Whatever model is used, it should be realistic and explain what women do and how they wish to be treated by men. The Basson model reflects how women wish to be treated. Dr. Chivers has shown that a woman can deny her own aroused body its proper expression while Dr. Amen has also shown why ANTs in the woman's mind can prevent intimacy from happening. These additional insights add to our understanding of why female sexual arousal may be difficult to approach with a simple pill.

Summary of 4 Models of Female Sexual Response
    Masters & Johnson (1966):
    Excitement/Arousal > Plateau> Orgasm>Resolution

    Kaplan (1979):
    Desire>Arousal>Orgasm

    Whipple & Brash-McGreer (1997):
    Desire>Excitement/Arousal/Plateau>Orgasm >Resolution

    Basson (2001):
    Sexual Stimulus + Emotional Connection > Arousal>Desire

Table 1. Summary 4 models of Female Sexual Arousal

	Phases				
	*SEDUCTION	*SENSATION	SURRENDER	*REFLECTION	
	1	2	3	4	5 or more?
Masters & Johnson 1966	Excitement/ Arousal	Plateau	Orgasm	Resolution	-
Kaplan, 1979	Desire	Arousal	Orgasm	-	-
*Whipple & Brash-McGreer, 1997	Desire	Excitement/ Arousal/ Plateau	Orgasm	Resolution	-
Basson, 2001	Stimulus + Emotional connection	Arousal	Desire	Excitement?	

*Represents the Reed model on which the Whipple/Brash-McGreer model is based. The Reed Model and consists of Seduction(desire), Sensations(excitement and plateau), Surrender(orgasm) and Reflection(Resolution).

The Whipple/Brash-McGreer (WBM) model also proposes that pleasure and satisfaction during one sexual experience can lead to the seduction phase of the next sexual experience. Notice that in all models except the Basson model, a sexual stimulus phase or component, the trigger for the sexual response, has been excluded. This is probably to simplify the otherwise complex steps in female sexual arousal. Since Basson has dived unabashedly into the complexity of the female response without trying to oversimplify in her model, she probably didn't mind including the sexual stimulus component in her model. A woman may stop at the excitement phase even though it is less likely. A man aroused to the excitement phase cannot stop. So when a woman stops at the excitement phase but the man cannot, rape can occur. So I would advise a man not to go to the aroused or excitement stage with a woman if he is not sure that she will allow both of them to go to the plateau and orgasm phase. If he fools himself into thinking he is good for the entire act, he may end up in jail for rape without intending to rape. Many men already are in jail for rape based on the woman's ability to stop at the excitement phase, a phase of no return for most men.

The Basson model shows that even when a woman is aroused and can derive physical satisfaction from the act, she may still be influenced by biological and psychological factors before going any further. She may say no at anytime along the entire phase. That's the message to all men, particularly single men. Perhaps rape can be defined as the lack of emotional intimacy preceding intercourse.

Figure 3: The Basson Model of Female Sexual Arousal.

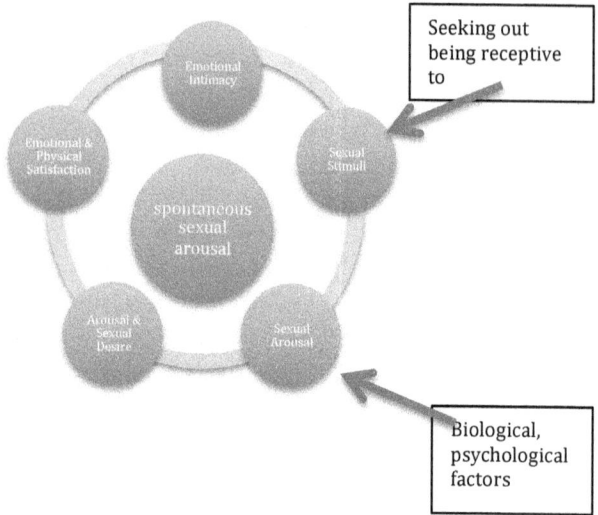

Seeking out being receptive to

Biological, psychological factors

Source: https://www.arhp.org/publications-and-resources/clinic-fact-sheets/female-sexual-response

These are the major factors involved in female sexual arousal and the female sexual response. Sexual stimulus does not just lead to female sexual arousal. A host of factors are involved. The time of the month, whether she is on her period, if she is happy or sad, how comfortable she is with the man, what happened the last time they were together all come into play. Many more factors drive a woman's sexual response than a man's.

The pill designed to increase arousal in women presumes that women respond sexually in a linear fashion. As you can see, a woman's sexual response is far from linear. I remember clearly joking to my wife about a man who has just gone to his parent's funeral and came back to the hotel and was aroused and ready to go. Three weeks later my father died. Two months later, during the funeral proceedings, it happened just like I predicted without realizing it. Men see sex as the thing that enables them to connect emotionally. A woman on the other hand needs to first feel an emotional connection even if she is aroused before sufficient desire for intercourse is generated. A woman may be physically aroused for sex but she also needs justification for engaging in it with her husband. Sounds crazy but that's only part of the complexity of the female sexual arousal response. For men, it is the physical sexual connection that gives them the feeling of an emotional connection. So while both husbands and wives need to connect emotionally in order to deepen the bond of love in their marriage, they approach this deepening from separate ends of a spectrum. The man comes from the purely physical end, the woman from the purely emotional end. They must meet in the middle and sex enables them to start right in the middle. In order for him to be emotionally sensitive and supportive, he must first connect to his wife sexually. If she doesn't allow him to connect sexually, he cannot continue to be emotionally available. If he is trying his best to connect to her emotionally despite not getting his own emotional nutrition through sexual intimacy, he will eventually become emotionally depleted. At some point, he may no longer be able to give his entire family the masculine type of emotional energy and support. His children may start seeing him as a wimp and may try to bring out the masculinity by breaking rules and boundaries. The emotionally spent father raises his children but leaves the impression on the children that they don't have a father. The latter can also occur in a household where the woman wants to be the boss in charge of everything because she makes more money, wants to always wear the pants, or has some undiagnosed psychiatric disorder. Women and their men must see that sex provides an effortless middle ground through which their love can be built to last. Sex is not just physical, it is emotional, mental, spiritual and according to the pornography industry, financial.

*Most nymphomaniacs are thought to be
plagued by a female orgasmic disorder.*

The psychological aspect plays a big role in female sexual arousal and Dr. Basson nailed it down to three major psychosocial issues: relationship satisfaction, self-image and sexual experiences. If a woman is satisfied about her relationship with her man, she may give in sexually, even if she is not in the mood. (Remember she may be aroused). If she isn't in the right mood, she may consider doing a favor depending on the marital state. Again, if she has a positive self-image, sees herself as hot and desirable, she may be willing and receptive. But even if she is the hottest commodity in the eyes of everyone else yet has a negative self-image, she may not be available. Thirdly, if her past sexual experience was a positive and thrilling one, it will make her more likely to be receptive.

Another reason I like the Basson model is because it clarifies that for women, the primary goal of sexual activity is not necessarily orgasm but personal satisfaction. This personal satisfaction is believed to manifest as physical satisfaction, orgasm, emotional satisfaction or increased intimacy with her partner. Summarized, the Basson model really let's us know that female sexual arousal does not begin with sexual stimuli but with emotional satisfaction.

Female sexual arousal begins with emotional intimacy. Male sexual arousal begins with sexual stimuli.

Many a man fantasize that if they were left stranded on an island with the most beautiful woman on earth, they would automatically have immediate access to her sexually since she has no other choice. Yet based on your knowledge of emotional intimacy as the first trigger, it is quite possible that a woman stranded on that man's fantasy island may not be sexually aroused because of a lack of an emotional connection.

In real life a woman wants to be wooed, desired and sought for like a priceless jewel. If you find a man still happily married today and enjoying perhaps even greater intimacy and bedroom privileges than when he first got married, you've found a man who knows something about wooing his wife. If you woo your wife and practice rule #3 in chapter 2, chances are high you'll be begging her to let you take a break. I said chances! Your ultimate goal during sexual intercourse is a female orgasm as the male more likely than not will reach an orgasm faster anyway. The male orgasm is unfortunately much cheaper. There are women who can orgasm by just thinking erotically and such orgasms do not involve the amygdala, the part of the brain that processes emotions and links them with long-term memory according to Rutgers University Professor Beverly Whipple. This may be the more evolved woman who has trained herself to orgasm so she not only enjoys erotic attention and intimacy and doesn't have to fake an orgasm.

WOMEN DENY THEIR AROUSAL STATES

Dr. Meredith Chivers studied straight and gay men and women and came up with reproducible and shocking realities about what arouses women. Subjects sat on a Lazyboy and were connected to gadgets one of which was a plethysmograph that measured blood flow and moistness in the vaginal walls while they watched erotic movie clips. The subjects were then asked to score their level of sexual arousal and record it on a keypad as they watched the movie clips. Women who claimed they were minimally aroused when watching some of the clips actually had measurements in the vagina that went through the roof. One conclusion to draw from this is that women often mask their levels of sexual arousal. Women need to understand and be more comfortable with their bodies. Wives who are more comfortable with their bodies enjoy more sex, passion and devotion from their husbands. They also experience the lasting love, peace, harmony and intimacy that a good marriage offers. More importantly, they are more likely to be financially successful because sex as the mind's greatest stimulant triggers more creativity and problem-solving strategies for life's challenges.

Chapter 6

LOW SEXUAL DESIRE

Hypoactive sexual desire disorder (HSDD), the original diagnosis for which the pink pill was tested was characterized by the absence of or reduced sexual fantasies or desire for sexual activity. This deficiency is not due to any mental, medical or medication-related condition and it may affect men or women. HSDD may be situational, that is the patient may only be disinterested in sexual activity with their current partner. It may be generalized, that is it is present regardless of having the right partner. HSDD can also be life long or it may be acquired, after a period of normal sexual function. Individuals with HSDD will not initiate or respond to their partner's sexual advances. It is a psychiatric diagnosis and was listed under the Sexual and Gender Identity Disorders section in the DSM-IV manual with a billing ICD-9 code of 302.71. In the more recent DSM-V, HSDD no longer exists. It has now been split into female sexual interest/arousal disorder (FSIAD) and male hypoactive sexual desire disorder (MHSDD). The ICD-10 billing code for both the male and female disorder is now F52.0. According to Kaplan's and Saddock's *Synopsis of Psychiatry*, prolonged abstinence from sex, hostility towards a partner, vagina dentata-(fear of vaginal castration, thanks Freud!), partner unavailability, health issues or erectile dysfunction may all lead to MHSDD. MHSDD is present in 6 percent of men aged 18-24 and 40% of men aged 65-74. A new cause of MHSDD is pornography addiction.

Female Sexual Interest/Arousal Disorder, FSIAD is defined as a lack of or significantly reduced sexual interest/arousal based on the six criteria below, lasting 6 months or longer and is not due to a nonsexual mental disorder, severe relationship distress, other significant stressors, drugs or other medical conditions.

DSM-V defines this more precisely as the presence of three or more of the following for 6 or more months:
1. Absent/reduced interest in sexual activity
2. Absent/reduced sexual/erotic thoughts or fantasies
3. No/reduced initiation of sexual activity, and typically unreceptive to a partner's attempts to initiate
4. Absent/reduced sexual excitement/pleasure during sexual activity in almost all or all (75-100% of sexual encounters
5. Absent/reduced sexual interest/arousal in response to any internal or external sexual/erotic cues(written, verbal, visual)
6. Absent/reduced genital or non-genital sensations during sexual activity in almost all or all sexual encounters.

The subtypes are similar to those for HSDD; lifelong or acquired, generalized or limited to specific situations and mild moderate or severe in terms of the accompanying associated distress. A woman having a distorted view of the female or male genitalia, perceiving the male tool as a weapon, too large or too small may also develop female sexual interest/arousal disorder. *(Kaplan & Saddock's Synopsis of Psychiatry. 11th Edition.)*

CAXTON'S SYNDROME

Caxton' Syndrome is low sexual desire in women or men accompanied by hostility in order to avoid sexual intimacy without any reason for the hostility. I have seen and now believe that there is another variant of low sexual desire disorder in women, one in which the women are intentionally hostile and not just disagreeable to their husband's sexual advances. This variant occurs in the absence of any trigger for hostility. The man has not done anything wrong but in order to hide her low sexual desire or fear of intimacy, the woman creates a constant war zone in the home. The hostility is usually directed at the husband around the time that sexual intimacy should occur in any other marriage or when the suggestion or possibility of sexual intimacy arises. The husband and wife may have left the kids at home, travelled to a different city and under normal circumstances have a romantic time together. The wife under those circumstances intentionally spoils the evening or moment by creating conflict in order to justify her subsequent hostility. When the man finally figures out that every time they have to be intimate, the wife starts a fight, he learns to tread softly. But he'll soon discover that treading softly does not change the wife's behavior; she always finds something to cause a fight when it's time to be intimate. On noticing the husband's wise approach, the wife may start accusing the husband of thinking she is crazy. "You think, I don't know what you're thinking, eh? I know you're thinking I'm crazy!" She starts fights so she can build up a hostile barrier to intimacy particularly sexual intimacy that eventually leads to counseling or complete marital breakup. Such couples may or may not have children and the man usually suffers from sexual deprivation. Caxton's Syndrome may be associated with PTSD secondary to childhood rape or some other trauma or prior negative events in the woman's life all of which are unrelated to anything the man has done. She would fight, attack, be disagreeable and all, usually around bedtime, just so she doesn't have to engage in sexual intimacy. She has no dyspareunia or any medical condition. For such women, there is no such thing as make-up sex. The hostile frigid wife probably has Caxton's Syndrome.

NO SEX AFTER MARRIAGE
Rarely, one may find an unconsummated marriage in which both partners never had sex in the marriage without having any inhibitions. They are simply unaware or simply put, "ignorant" of what to do. They have no underlying physical or mental illness. They may be afraid. The duration of this condition does not determine the prognosis according to the 11th edition of *Kaplan & Saddock's Synopsis of Psychiatry*. They can be taught what to do and they would learn to enjoy each other afterwards.

NO ORGASMS?

52

There is a female orgasmic disorder in which women engaging in sexual activity do not achieve orgasm, have delayed orgasm or one that is of markedly reduced intensity. The women experience distress as a result of this inability. They have delayed or infrequent orgasms 75 to 100% of the time during sexual intercourse. A greater proportion of women get more orgasms during intercourse as they get older. This may be because of greater experience or lesser inhibition. This begs the question of whether women really teach each other (mother-daughter) these things at the right time. While a woman may enjoy intimacy without having an orgasm, women who don't reach orgasm may be easily frustrated, highly irritable or have psychosomatic pelvic pains with no organic basis. They may avoid sexual intimacy or any form of intimacy altogether. The woman who is always busy serving or working outside the home but cannot sit at home and enjoy her husband and family during the holidays may be such a woman. She will not stay home and enjoy intimacy with her husband during the holidays. She can be found travelling every holiday to see mom, dad, uncle, aunt, nephew or niece but leaves her own husband at home. The husband may have gone along at first, but with his own busy schedule he soon realizes it's better to rest at home during the vacation and enjoy his wife's company. The wife, suffering from Intimacy Avoidance Disorder (IAD) then proposes a vacation trip. She knows it's resting time for the man and wants to escape. As she becomes more proficient at hiding her intimacy avoidant disorder or FSIAD, she learns to make her husband feel guilty for not going with her and at the same time "forgive" him for not traveling. Those moments where ordinarily a normal woman will stay home and just spend the time with her husband. She refuses to be intimate with her loving emotionally spent husband. IAD is far more common in men than in women.

TOO MANY ORGASMS!

There are two psychiatric diagnoses, Persistent Genital Arousal Disorder (PGAD) and Female Premature Orgasm in which women are hyper-aroused. Is that good for the woman or her husband? Let's look at the definitions first. In PGAD, women have continuous sexual arousal that according to *Kaplan and Saddock's Synopsis of Psychiatry* is "uncomfortable, demands release and interferes with life pleasures and activities". Its cause is unknown and the women masturbate incessantly because orgasm provides temporary relief. They seek orgasms constantly because it is the only thing that provides them with temporary relief. Sex for them is no longer a pleasure but a desperate necessity for obtaining temporary relief from the hyper-aroused state.

The other hyper-aroused state in women is called Female Premature Orgasm (FPO). Women with Female Premature Orgasm have multiple spontaneous orgasms without sexual stimulation. Cases of yawning-induced orgasms have been reported in patients on Prozac even though it is well known to cause reduced libido and absent orgasms.

In closing, there is a tall order of both natural and artificial barriers that Pink has to overcome in order to be the pill men and women dream the pill would be. First of all keep in mind that women just have a natural tendency to want to avoid sexual intimacy. Perhaps it's a preserving natural instinct. The pregnancy period is a vulnerable period for every woman. The instinct to avoid sex may prevent an unwanted pregnancy, unnecessary vulnerability or dependency, particularly in a world hostile to women. In a dog-eat-dog world, the comforting assurance of a loving husband and secure protective home may be a necessity before a woman in her right mind can feel free enough to be sexual. But there are many who have all these and still refuse to be intimate with their husbands. Can Pink override these natural instincts in a woman? If it can, wouldn't that turn it into an advanced date rape drug? There are additional intrinsic and extrinsic barriers that pink has to overcome. What are some of these barriers? Intrinsic factors include gender identity issues, malicious withholding, medical illness, recent injury or surgery. Extrinsic factors include a non-conducive environment such as kids sleeping nearby, lack of privacy, emotional triggers such as a recent fight, arguments or lack of seduction and education on the part of both partners.

If you want your wife to be a passionate animal when in bed with you, stop behaving like an animal outside the bedroom.

PART 2

THE PINK PILL

The pink pill flibanserin marketed as Addyi® was released in pharmacies nationwide on October 17, 2015 for treating FSIAD. Multiple aspects of this drug from the concept of its development to its time of approval make it a truly interesting drug. That the drug is on the market today reflects how consumer groups can ignore the scientific facts of a study and push powerful government entities such as the FDA in the wrong direction. It seems if you want to get anything these days, all you need do is accuse others of sexism, racism or homophobia. The first one, sexism, was used to force the hand of the FDA to approve Pink. Viagra became a blockbuster drug because of its simple effectiveness for a simple-minded process, male performance, not arousal. Men are easily and readily aroused and spend more time thinking about sex. We are wired that way. Women are not wired that way as you saw in the Arousal section in earlier chapters.

This section addresses concerns and safety issues as well as the overall impact the drug Flibanserin might have on female psychiatry, the female psych, the practice of medicine, psychiatry and marriages on the brink of collapse due to sexual deprivation and starvation. But first, lets deal with the ...

Chapter 7

FDA "SEXISM" CONTROVERSY

Pink, flibanserin would be the first drug ever approved by the FDA for increasing either male or female sexual desire. It is unlikely that pink with its poor efficacy and serious side effects outweighing benefits would have been approved by the FDA had it not been the push from consumer advocate groups. Some of these groups accused the FDA of sexism. Other groups did not want the drug approved based on the scientific data Sprout Pharmaceutical provided to the FDA. The "sexism" accusation of the FDA was sponsored by the pharmaceutical industry. Accusing the FDA of sexism in the case of flibanserin is ridiculous for several reasons. First, men think about sex so much more than women. We like sex. If a pill would increase the desire for sex in women, why would men, presumed to be the majority in the FDA approval panel for Pink, not approve the drug? Secondly, Pink has dangerous side effects. Thirdly you will soon see from the FDA documents, Pink has little evidence of benefit when compared with placebo clinically. Most men would be glad to have a pill that increases their female partner's arousal. Several of the men I have counseled in the past barely get enough "cookies" from their spouse in a year and they would celebrate this drug wholeheartedly. So, no, I don't think sexism was a factor in denying approval for this drug by presumed "chauvinistic" FDA staff in either 2010 when Boehringer-Ingelheim gave flibanserin up to the Whiteheads or in 2013 when it was denied approval again. If anything, men would push for the drug to be approved so they can get more action. I think it was the clinical trial data and the science behind it that led to these denials. What the consumer advocates have done regarding this drug is to push women backwards rather than forwards with the unnecessary demand that the drug be approved. On June 4, 2015, Flibanserin was approved with an 18:6 vote in favor of approval. Such votes are usually unanimous when there is convincing evidence regarding safety and efficacy.

When a drug is approved for a specific indication, that indication must be a condition with a crystal clear definition and clear-cut diagnostic criteria. The original diagnosis for which Sprout pharmaceutical sought approval, Hypoactive Sexual Desire Disorder, HSDD, no longer exists. According to an article by Diana Zuckerman, President of the *National Center for Health Research* and Judy Norsinian, co-founder and past executive director of *Our Bodies Ourselves* accused the FDA of caving in to consumer advocacy groups in approving Addyi®. Non-profit organizations such as *Even the Score* were funded by pharmaceutical companies including Sprout Pharmaceuticals for the "sexist" campaign against the FDA. Whether there was a sound basis for the campaign will be something for you to judge when you look at all the clinical trial evidence. Sifting through all the data provided during clinical trials can be quite intimidating. It's therefore no surprise that even the FDA and Valeant, the company that eventually purchased flibanserin for a billion dollars from Sprout, missed the most important data of the trial results. You are about to see how the results submitted by Sprout to both the FDA and perhaps the company that bought Addyi® do not meet the expected requirements.

Chapter 8

HOW PINK WAS BORN

Pink, flibanserin was originally developed and presented to the FDA as a potential antidepressant. It however failed to meet the criteria for efficacy as an antidepressant during the efficacy trials. It was then noted that the subjects on Pink did not have sexual dysfunction, a typical adverse effect associated with antidepressant drugs. Thus began the determination to find a good use for Pink with respect to sexual function. You might be thinking if there is a drug such as Viagra® for men, why isn't there one for women? There should be a drug for every ailment for women if one does exist for men. That's only fair. The way Viagra® works however is pure science with clinically proven irrefutable and reproducible evidence. Paralyzed male patients with spinal cord injury unable to have an erection for months or years since their injury were able to do so when given Viagra. In one study of 41 spinal cord injury patients treated with Sildenafil (Viagra, blue pill), 93% had a positive response sufficient to allow sexual intercourse. This article published in the August 2000 edition of the journal of *European Urology* is just one of many such articles on the efficacy of the blue pill. Data on Pink is not that scientifically convincing. I don't think anyone goes out of their way to prevent a drug from being approved for women's health. Yet this is the very thing the FDA was accused of by the Sprout funded non-profit organizations that accused the FDA of "sexism". Daniel Bergner, author of *What Do Women Want*, wrote that "…women's sexual problems usually aren't genital; they're entrenched in psychological complexities." Until these complexities are duly addressed, nothing can really work without becoming a date rape drug. You saw the nature of these complexities in the previous section.

> ***Women's sexual problems aren't usually genital but psychological***

THE FDA NEW DRUG APPROVAL PROCESS
Every consumer who takes a pill ought to have an idea how the pill they pop into their mouth came to be. You can visit www.fdareview.org published by *The Independent Institute,* to learn more. It is a great website for browsing about drug development.

Drug development and market approval are very rigorous and expensive processes. There are basically four phases an approved drug goes through in order to reach the market. Prior to finding a potential drug with a likelihood of getting to the market, drug manufacturers synthesize, purify and test thousands of different compounds. About 0.1 percent or one in every one thousand compounds so tested will appear promising enough to enter into the drug-testing phase. This drug-testing phase requires FDA approval. To get this approval, the drug company must file an *Investigational New Drug* (IND) application with the

FDA. Once approved, the company then proceeds to the development phase of the drug. This development occurs in four progressive phases called clinical trials. Each phase has its own overall likelihood of failure, and success, costs and time constraints all well charted according to Dimasi, Hansen and Grabowski on the www.fdareview.org website. In all the four phases of drug development, safety must be determined. In the different phases, drug tolerability, toxicity, side effects and optimal dosages are determined. Only 30 percent of drugs will make it to Phase I of the study and 14 percent of these will make it to Phase II. Of the drugs that make it to Phase II, 9 percent will reach Phase III. Only 8 percent of the Phase III drugs will get approved via FDA's New Drug Application (NDA) process. Phase I is for safety only and helps determine the drug's basic properties as well as its safety in healthy individuals. Phase II determines safety, dosing and efficacy. Phase III is to determine safety, efficacy and side effects using randomized double-blind placebo controlled trials and is the most expensive of the three, sometimes costing close to $90 million. An average of ten years and about $120 million dollars is involved in the development of a new drug and obtaining final FDA approval. When a company files the final NDA, the FDA must respond within 60 days. There, now you know something about how drugs reach your local pharmacy!

HOW DOES THE PINK PILL WORK?

Frankly, no one knows how Pink works. It is not in any specific drug class. Had it been approved when

Boerhinger-Ingelheim had it in their stalls and sought approval for it as an antidepressant, it would have been classified as an antidepressant. That would immediately have placed it in the same family as Trazodone and nefazodone. It wasn't. So asides from its long chemical name, it dangles as an orphan with the chemical formula $C_{20}H_{21}F_3N_4O$. Its IUPAC name (International Union of Physics and Chemistry) is 1-2-{4-[3-(Trifluoromethyl)phenyl]-1-piperazinyl}ethyl)-1,3 dihydro-2H-benzimidazol-2-one. (ACD/IUPAC). The chemical structure of Pink is very similar to that of trazodone with a chemical formula of $C_{19}H_{22}Cl_2N_5O$. For those who hate chemistry, particularly organic chemistry, never mind. Just see the structure of both Pink and Trazodone below as 3 hexagons (6 sides) and one pentagon (5 sides) linked by "N"s with an O at the end of the pentagon. That's all. Pretend as if you are looking at the Sunday morning paper cartoon section while trying to "spot the differences". If the structures appear similar, it means you do know some chemistry.

TRAZODONE, THE FIRST COUSIN OF FLIBANSERIN

Since we cannot at the present time pin down flibanserin to any specific drug class, I would classify it along its closest chemical relative drug, Trazodone as an antidepressant. Approved by the FDA as an antidepressant in 1982, Trazodone is a serotonin uptake inhibitor and is used as an antidepressant particularly in patients with anxiety or difficulty sleeping. Trazodone is the closest chemical compound to flibanserin and hopefully, you can see the similarities between Pink and

Trazodone in the imbedded picture below. One of the side effects of Trazodone is priapism, a prolonged erection in men that is not due to sexual stimuli. Whether this priapism has anything to do with its chemical relative flibanserin's causing a supposed increase in sexual arousal or desire in women remains unclear and may be a good research question.

Figure 4. Chemical structure of Flibanserin & Trazodone

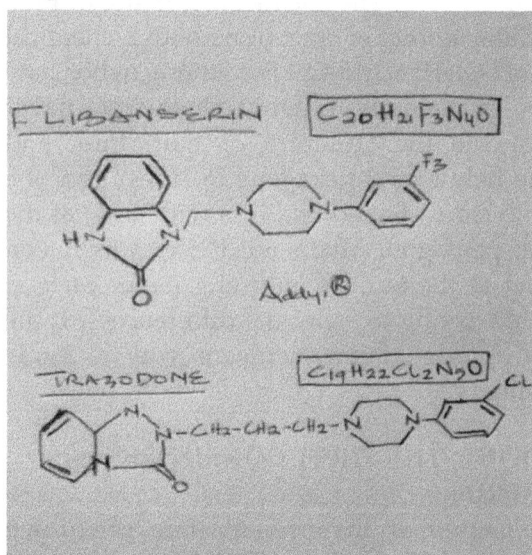

Do you think they look alike? Can you spot the differences?

INDICATION FOR FLIBANSERIN

Flibanserin has only one indication, FSIAD. Flibanserin was originally tested as a drug indicated for Hypoactive Sexual Desire Disorder (HSDD) in premenopausal women. As mentioned earlier, this diagnosis no longer exists and HSDD has now come under the umbrella of Female Sexual Interest/Arousal Disorder. Female Sexual Arousal Disorder by itself, also known as Candace Syndrome, is associated with the inability or difficulty remaining aroused until the completion of sexual activity. Pink is indicated for Female Sexual Interest/Arousal Disorder and this is a psychiatric diagnosis. If you're on flibanserin, you do have a psychiatric diagnosis, whether you'd like to admit it or not.

You may skip this next chapter on pharmacology if you're not interested in the behavior of the drug or the clinical trials leading to the approval of the drug by the FDA.

Chapter 9

PHARMACOLOGY OF FLIBANSERIN

The chemical formula for pink is $C_{20}H_{21}F_3N_4O$. It has a molecular mass of 390.4g/mol. Pink, according to the FDA documents from the parent company Sprout Pharmaceuticals, displays a linear and dose proportional pharmacokinetics after single oral doses as low as 0.5mg to 150mg and after multiple oral doses ranging from 60mg to 300mg daily. Steady state levels are achieved in about three days. Pink is rapidly absorbed with 90% of the dose reaching the bloodstream as flibanserin or its metabolites. Maximum plasma concentrations are reached within 45 to 60 minutes after oral administration and the absolute bioavailability of the drug is 33%. Food affects peak plasma concentrations of flibanserin prolonging the time to peak plasma concentrations from about 60 minutes to between 105 minutes and 4 hours. The mean terminal half-life of Pink after oral administration once it has reached steady state levels in the plasma is 12 hours. It is excreted after oxidative metabolism by CYP3A4 and CYP2D6 cytochrome P450 isoenzymes. The liver excretes about 51% while the kidneys excretes about 44% of the drug. When Pink was given with ketoconazole, a strong CYP3A4 inhibitor, its levels increased 4.5 fold. When Pink was administered along with fluconazole, a moderate inhibitor of CYP3A4 isoenzymes, flibanserin levels increased 7-fold.

The first in its class as an approved drug for sexual arousal, was initially investigated as a potential antidepressant. Pink has a preferential affinity for serotonin 5-HT(1A) serotonin 5-HT(2A) receptors and binds equally to both receptors. At higher levels of 5-HT such as when under stress, pink may occupy more 5-HT (2A) receptors than 5-HT(1A) receptors. Flibanserin also has a similar affinity for dopamine D(4k) receptors. It acts as an agonist on 5-HT(1A) receptors, an antagonist on 5-HT(2A) receptors and as a weak agonist on dopamine D(4) receptors. Its agonist effects on 5-HT(1A) and D4 receptors, was initially published by Dr. Borsini and colleagues in the summer 2002 issue of the *Journal of CNS Drug Review*. Dr. Borsini has studied flibanserin and published extensively on its central nervous system effects mostly in rats. Pink reduces firing rates in nerve cells of the dorsal raphe, hippocampus and cortex with the CA1 region being the most sensitive region in the brain. This pink-induced firing rate in the cortex is thought by Dr. Borsini to be mediated through stimulation of post-synaptic 5-HT(1A) receptors, whereas the reduction in the number of active firing cells in the dorsal raphe seems to be mediated through dopamine D(4) receptor stimulation. Pink quickly desensitizes somatic 5-HT autoreceptors in the dorsal raphe and enhances tonic activation of postsynaptic 5-HT(1A) receptors in the CA3 region. Pink also preferentially reduces synthesis and extracellular levels of 5-HT in the cortex, where it enhances extracellular levels of norepinephrine and dopamine. Flibanserin showed antidepressant activity in animals sensitive to antidepressants and did so by acting directly or indirectly via stimulation of 5-HT(1A), dopamine, and opioid receptors. Pink induces sedation. For more information, read *Pharmacology of Flibanserin* by Borsini F, Evans K, Jason K, Rohde F, Alexander B, Pollentier S published in the *Summer 2002* issue of *CNS Drug Review*. Dr. Borsini had shown earlier in an article published in the September 1999 issue of the journal of *Pharmacology Biochemistry & Behavior* that Pink induced hypermotility in mice and rats at 4-mg/kg, anxiolytic-like effects at 8-16mg/kg as well as antagonizing the d-amphetamine and apomorphine-induced stereotypy in rats. At 16mg/kg, Pink reduced spontaneous motor activity in rats.

In another article published by Dr. Invernizzi and colleagues in the *British Journal of Pharmacology* in August 2003, Pink lowered brain levels of 5-HT and raised dopamine and noradrenaline levels in the rat prefrontal cortex.

Let's quit this thick jungle of technical material by simply summarizing that flibanserin acts as an agonist on 5-HT(1A) receptors, an antagonist on 5-HT(2A) receptors and as a weak agonist on dopamine D(4) receptors. Never mind what these mean if you're not in love with science or chemistry. All it means is that the Pink, like most drugs that work in the brain, are attracted to certain well-known receptor sites in the brain.

REAL CHALLENGES FROM PREDICTABLE POTENTIAL SIDE EFFECTS OF PINK

Physicians prescribing Pink as well as the patient who uses this drug should consider the real life-threatening danger that may be associated with using this drug. Looking at the proposed receptors on which Flibanserin acts, quite similar to those of Trazodone, one can predict it would have a similar side effect profile like Trazodone. Trazodone is a direct 5-HT2A and 5-HT2C receptor antagonist and a weak serotonin reuptake inhibitor. Trazodone causes significant orthostatic hypotension via its alpha-adrenergic antagonist effect, as well as priapism, the latter occurring in 1 out of every 10,000 men on the drug. Trazodone has also been associated with an increased risk of arrhythmias in patients with mitral valve prolapse or premature ventricular contractions. The typical side effects of Trazodone include, dizziness, nausea, headache and orthostatic hypotension. In the clinical trials, flibanserin caused significant orthostatic hypotension, dizziness and sedation. These side effects are typical for both Trazodone and Nefazodone, another heterocyclic antidepressant. Perhaps based on its similar side effect profile with the Trazodone-nefazodone group, one can postulate that flibanserin may share similar side effects with nefazodone; dizziness, weakness, headache, dry mouth, nausea and constipation. If one were to therefore lump Pink with any established class of drugs, it would be with the second-generation serotonin reuptake inhibitor antidepressants trazodone and the third-generation serotonin reuptake inhibitor antidepressant nefazodone. When you look at their chemical structures, the similarity becomes more striking. This then raises concerns about patients on Pink developing antidepressant withdrawal syndrome.

Antidepressant Discontinuation Syndrome

Patients on trazodone and possibly Pink, may develop signs and symptoms of the antidepressant withdrawal syndrome. These include flu-like symptoms, insomnia, nausea, imbalance, sensory disturbances and hyper-arousal (FINISH). FINISH occurs in approximately 20 percent of patients following abrupt discontinuation of an antidepressant that was taken for at least six weeks. The symptoms are usually mild, last one to two weeks and quickly resolve if the antidepressant is restarted. This syndrome was well described in an article published in the *American Family Physician* in August 2006 by Major Christopher Warner et al. While no such reports were reported directly from the Pink trials, it should be an intelligently anticipated possibility since its chemical structure and pharmacological profile is similar to that of trazodone (Desyrel). As an atypical antidepressant, Trazodone withdrawal symptoms can occur even though such withdrawal symptoms are commoner in selective serotonin reuptake inhibitors (SSRIs) and those with a short half-life. Trazodone has an elimination half-life of about 10 hours and a redistribution half-life of about one hour.

I found a few interesting comments reported on trazodone withdrawal in patients on the website

70

www.drugs.com. One patient tapered off trazodone from 50 to 25mg to 0 in three days and felt better with just a few weeks of some "shakiness". Another patient on 300mg daily who had his medication discontinued developed seizures. Another individual took trazodone for 10 years, went from 300mg to 200mg for three years, quit cold turkey and experienced symptoms she described as zombie–like. One individual had bed-soaking night sweats requiring bedding change in the middle of the night after discontinuing Trazodone. Trazodone is known to prolong the QT/QTc interval and may thereby lead to cardiovascular complications including dizziness, fainting and arrhythmias. Torsades de pointes has been reported in the immediate release form even at doses of 100mg per day. I think electrolytes and liver function should be checked in patients before and during use of Pink. I suspect that an EKG may also be needed before starting the pink pill or sometime after initiating treatment. Despite the similar side-effect profile with trazodone which prolongs QT intervals, the clinical trials and therefore the manufacturers do not suggest that we should obtain an EKG, blood chemistry profile or hydration levels in patients on Pink. Why not? Could the dizziness, orthostatic hypotension and syncope experienced by patients on Pink be due to transient torsades or QT/QTc prolongation? Maybe. Acute angle closure glaucoma, hyponatremia, priapism, worsening suicide risk, neuroleptic malignant syndrome and serotonergic syndrome are all associated with trazodone use. These side effects should therefore all be anticipated in the pink pill.

OTHER SIDE EFFECTS PREDICTED FOR PINK

These other side effect predictions are based on the behaviors of known medications with similar receptor affinity or chemical structure.

5-HT Receptor Effects

As a practicing physician, I have seen, evaluated admitted and treated depressed patients attempting suicide or simply tired of life. They seem to recycle through the same emergency rooms and psychiatric inpatient facilities from month to month despite the multiple drugs prescribed for them. Depression is a symptom of an underlying problem deep within the soul of the individual. So far, there isn't any known drug designed to cater to the deepest needs of the human soul. I believe that's why there won't be a pill to cure depression. The day you find one and it doesn't have an element of psychotherapy, hope or placebo attached to it, you have a magic pill worthy of a Nobel Prize.

Flibanserin like its cousin Trazodone and based on its first investigational new drug application is expected to behave like an antidepressant influencing 5-HT receptors. If it works there will still be safer alternatives. Though Pink lacked efficacy as an antidepressant, its mechanism of receptor-related function remains similar to that of Trazodone. Antidepressants are not as effective as presumed according to a study published in the August 3, 1996 issue of the *British Medical Journal*

(BMJ). In a pooled study of 1757 patients conducted in Germany, St. Johns wort (*Hypericum perforatum*), a herb with antibacterial, antioxidant anti-inflammatory and antiviral properties was found to be superior to placebo and as effective as antidepressants in the treatment of mild and moderate depression. St. Johns wort also had fewer side effects compared with antidepressants. It is now indicated for the treatment of mild to moderate depression in Germany. Germans have a good taste not only for beer and cars, but also for medicines that work. When the St. Johns wort study was repeated in the United States in 2001 according to Robert Whitaker author of *Anatomy of An Epidemic*, only 15 percent of the St. Johns wort and only 5 percent of the placebo patients respectively improved. When another NIH funded study comparing the effects of St. Johns wort with Zoloft were published in 2002 in the *Journal of the American Medical Association (JAMA)*, St. John's wort was found to be "no better than placebo". This study was the joint effort of the *National Center for Complementary and Alternative Medicine (NCCAM), National Institute of Mental Health (NIMH)* and the *Office of Dietary Supplements (ODS)*. About 24 percent of depressed patients taking St. Johns wort, 25 percent of those taking Zoloft, and 32 percent of those on placebo responded fully to their treatment, according to the press release from the NIH dated April 9, 2002 from the NCCAM and NIMH offices. This meant that placebo was not only better than St. John's wort, it was also better than Zoloft by a whopping 28 percent. The study might as well have concluded that *Zoloft was no better than placebo or St. John's wort*. Antidepressants increase the risk of suicide in depressed patients. So if depression accompanies FSIAD and is not properly addressed, flibanserin, acting as a poor antidepressant, may worsen the depression or precipitate suicide in women.

DOPAMINE AGONIST EFFECTS

Predicting the dopaminergic effects of flibanserin without clinical trial details is almost impossible. This is because dopamine affects multiple functions in the body including motor function, the stress response and addictive behavior. In addition, patients with life-threatening shock from either overwhelming infection, heart block, cardiac arrest or blood loss can be resuscitated with high infusions of dopamine. It is the chemical involved in addiction to cocaine, heroine and methadone. The dopamine D4 receptor (DRD4) is the target for drug treatment of schizophrenia and Parkinson's disease. The DRD4-7R (7-repeat) variant has also been linked to ADHD. More specifically, children with the DRD4-7R genotype require higher doses of methylphenidate, (trade name Adderal®) according to the December 2004 *Journal of Child & Adolescent Psychopharmacology* article published by Dr. Stephanie Hamarman and colleagues.

Dopamine agonists such as levodopa and ropinirole are used in the treatment of Parkinson's and restless leg. These drugs are known to cause orthostatic hypotension, hallucination, hypersexuality, impulse control problems such as compulsive shopping, compulsive eating and pathological gambling. To avoid these side effects

74

in the dopamine agonists, they have to be tapered. Sometimes however tapering results in dopamine agonist withdrawal syndrome (DAWS). The symptoms of DAWS include anxiety, agitation, panic attacks, depression, drug craving, fatigue, generalized pain, suicide ideation, nausea, orthostatic hypotension, sweating and vomiting. Most importantly, there is no known treatment for DAWS at this time. So while flibanserin is considered a weak dopamine D4 agonist, it may still result in the same side effects as stronger dopamine agonists as well as side effects from its withdrawal, DAWS. You must keep them in mind.

Overall, the side effects of flibanserin including mice breast tumor development and appendicitis make it a truly interesting drug to observe as it goes though its post-marketing phase.

Chapter 10

FDA ATTACKS THE PINK PILL

This chapter deals with some of the scientific facts behind the rejection of flibanserin as a drug for sexual arousal disorder. It also addresses some concerns and controversies. Female sexuality is more complex compared with male sexuality. For that same reason, sexual arousal and desire in women are not easy to evaluate in clinical trials. Nevertheless, a scientific method was applied in procuring the data.

First let's look briefly at the clinical trial design from a simplified angle. When a drug is being tested for an application, the drug must accomplish something. That "something" would either be a primary end point or secondary end point. The FDA and the drug company must both agree on these endpoints. Unlike a drug for hypertension with well-defined endpoints established by cardiologists, a new drug whose class and intended effects are uncertain may require multiple meetings between drug manufacturer and the FDA to determine specific end points. Multiple meetings preceded the New Drug Application (NDA) of Pink in 2009.

Both parties agreed on two co-primary endpoints and one secondary endpoint for the Phase III drug development trials. The two primary endpoints were (1)A change from baseline in the number of satisfying sexual events (SSEs) and (2) a change from baseline in sexual desire recorded in an electronic diary (eDiary). The secondary endpoint was to measure the change in distress associated with reduced sexual desire following treatment with Pink. The latter, distress, was one of the criteria for the original definition of hypoactive sexual desire disorder (HSDD) before DSM-V.

So summarily the phase III trials were designed to evaluate these three endpoints:

1. Satisfying Sexual Events (SSEs)
2. Sexual Desire
3. Distress

Now the real drama begins to unfold.

On January 8, 2009, Boehringer-Ingelheim had a meeting with the FDA and informed them that there was a problem; the second primary endpoint sexual desire recorded by participants in the eDiary in two of the three pivotal phase 3 primary efficacy trials (Study 511.71 and Study 511.75) were not statistically significant. Boehringer-Ingelheim officials told the FDA that participants had decreased compliance with daily diary entry over time. Usually that either meant that the pharmaceutical company would have to repeat the trials, cancel the entire trial if they suspect that the outcome would be poor overall or extend the duration of the trials. But Boehringer-Ingelheim blamed the poor compliance of participants in completing the daily eDiary entry to "diary fatigue". The rigor of science when the safety of the general population is at stake demands that such "diary fatigue" be anticipated before hand and be adequately addressed in the clinical trial design. That may mean daily reminder calls or electronic prompts to participants. Today such reminder calls to clinical trial participants can be automated and done through a simple smart phone app. As a pharmaceutical company interested in delivering safe effective drugs to the general public, they did have the resources and responsibility to employ such technology if they so desired. Instead, Boehringer-Ingelheim suggested that rather than the agreed upon daily eDiary, the FDA should allow them to use the two questions from the desire domain of the Female Sexual Function Index (FSFI) to assess desire.

That is a problem in itself because the FSFI questionnaire assesses interest over a 28-day period. To use this FSFI instrument, the ability of patients to recall other events during the same period must first be tested. If they cannot be trusted to accurately recall certain events during the same period, then the FSFI questionnaire cannot be trusted as a valid instrument for measuring sexual function.

At best, it may provide a statistically significant difference between Pink and placebo but not a clinically significant one. Clinically it is obvious that even the brightest patients would not be able to recall the same amount of information in 28 days that they would have in 24 hours! Yet for some strange reason that no one can explain, after Boehringer-Ingelheim informed the FDA on January 8 that although the phase 3 Study 511.71 and Study 511.75 did not produce statistically significant efficacy, they requested the use of a less reliable tool. This would further dilute the clinical significance and relevance of the trials. Dr. Bertram Spilker, one of the foremost authorities on clinical trial designs stated that

> "An efficacy test that demonstrates a 10% change after medicine treatment may be statistically significant, but a change of 50% may be required for the results to be clinically significant (clinically meaningful). " - *Guide to Clinical Trials.* Bert Spilker. Raven Press, New York. 1991. p. 82

Following Dr. Spilker's cue, if a medicine under investigation docs not produce a statistically significant change in the efficacy primary end point, then it probably doesn't stand a chance clinically. Rather than intensify the methods of ensuring patient compliance with the more accurate daily eDiary in their trials, Boehringer-Ingelheim wanted the FDA to bypass sound protocols for an easier option. It's quite obvious that the daily e-Diary records would be more accurate than a tool such as the FSFI that allows you to guess and try to recall what happened 4 weeks ago. Naturally, the FDA refused, stating that the FSFI-desire component had questionable validity and recall bias, after all how many people remember what they ate for dinner four nights ago! How about 4 weeks ago? The 28-day recall may be useful for marriage therapists trying to get a general idea about a marital issue. But such a long recall period is basically useless in drug efficacy trials where hard objective data are needed. Our memory is just not that good over a 4-week period! FSFI is good for overall perception evaluation by marriage therapists but cannot be used as a reliable tool for hard science efficacy numbers if proper daily documentation is not done.

Nine and a half months later on October 27, 2009, Boehringer-Ingelheim filed a new drug application, NDA 022526 seeking authorization for flibanserin for the treatment of hypoactive sexual desire disorder (HSDD) in premenopausal women. About eight months after this filing on June 18, 2010, at the FDA's *Reproductive Health Drugs Advisory Committee* meeting, the Committee was asked what they thought about changing the co-primary endpoint. Nine out of 11 did not agree with changing the co-primary endpoint and all eleven voted unanimously not to recommend approval of Pink for HSDD treatment in premenopausal women. The reason for this was simple. Pink had not demonstrated an acceptable overall benefit-to-risk profile in the study participants.

On July 22, 2010, about 6 weeks later at the *post-Advisory Committee* meeting, the FDA met with Boehringer-Ingelheim and informed them of the need to address several issues. First, Boehringer-Ingelheim must show sufficient proof that the FSFI-desire instrument had content validity, recall validity as well as clarification on the measurement properties of the FSFI. Secondly, Boehringer-

Ingelheim needed to show additional efficacy data in real patients who may have co-morbid illnesses, particularly those on concomitant medications that had been excluded from their previous trials. To all these, Boehringer-Ingelheim officials responded that they were already conducting Study 511.147, initiated in 2009 and that it was using the FSFI-desire items as a pre-specified co-primary endpoint. So now Boehringer-Ingelheim is using a less accurate instrument that would be blurry at best in pointing towards the efficacy of Pink by changing from a daily eDiary with the highest accuracy of recall to a monthly one.

On August 27, 2010, Boehringer-Ingelheim received a letter called a *Complete Response* (CR) letter from the FDA. This letter listed the safety, clinical efficacy and pharmacological deficiencies and what the FDA wanted: (1) re-analysis of the studies using the FSFI-desire endpoint, (2) an additional trial with the FSFI-desire items as a pre-specified co-primary efficacy endpoint, as well as additional studies (3) to demonstrate the effect of co-administration of 100mg flibanserin with moderate CYP3A4 inhibitors such as fluconazole, moderate CYP3A4 inducers such as modafinil and alcohol, (4) evaluating the risks of syncope-related events using supra-therapeutic (extremely high doses) of flibanserin and (5) the abuse potential of flibanserin.

A silent gap existed for almost 2 years during which Sprout Pharmaceutical acquired all rights to flibanserin from Boehringer-Ingelheim in 2012. Following the acquisition, a pre-NDA meeting was held between Sprout and the FDA on April 26, 2012. Sprout was informed at the meeting that the appropriateness of the FSFI-desire domain for evaluating sexual desire would be assessed whenever Sprout Pharmaceuticals responded to the August 27, 2010 *Complete Response* letter received by Boehringer-Ingelheim. Sprout submitted their response to the August 27, 2010 FDA letter on March 29, 2013. The FDA countered this response by sending a second CR letter to Sprout Pharmaceuticals on September 27, 2013. That letter again requested that Sprout address (1) the validity concerns of the FSFI-desire domain, (2) perform a dedicated driving simulation study to evaluate the potential for next day impairment after nighttime use of Pink in drivers, (3) safety issues such as rare incidence of appendicitis, (4) additional drug-drug interactions as well as (5) the clinical risk of breast cancer in light of the dose-related mammary tumors found in mice.

These are genuine safety concerns from an institution meant to protect the public. Wouldn't you expect Sprout to respond to these requests? How do you think they responded? Sprout responded not by providing safety or efficacy data as requested but by filing a Formal Dispute Resolution Request (FDRR) with the Office of New Drugs (OND) on December 3, 2013. Sprout asked OND to approve flibanserin for HSDD without requiring additional data. Bold, isn't it? The OND Director Dr. Jenkins sent a denial on February 7, 2014, a week before Valentine's Day on the ground that the benefits of pink do not outweigh its side-effects. He also demanded that the previously requested items be submitted. Sprout complied and met with the FDA again on January 15, 2015 and stated they would submit data for a third review cycle.

Chapter 11

PINK CLINICAL TRIAL DETAILS

Seven Phase 3 clinical studies were performed and only three of them were considered as meeting the optimal study design criteria outlined by the FDA. These are studies 511.71 (US & Canada), 511.75 (US & Canada) and 511.147 (US only). These three pivotal trials were randomized double-blinded, North American studies in premenopausal women with acquired HSDD. Of the 3,548 female patients 18 years or older randomized to treatment, 2,310 were randomized to flibanserin and 1,238 were randomized to placebo. The overall completion rate was 70% in the flibanserin group and 78% in the placebo group. The FDA reported that efficacy data from two of the Study 511.75 sites involving 69 patients were excluded from FDA analyses due to data integrity issues.

ADDITIONAL ELIGIBILITY CRITERIA:

All the women in the study were generally healthy and in a stable monogamous heterosexual relationship for at least one year prior to the screening. The partner was expected to be physically present for at least 50% of each month during the screening period and the 24-week efficacy period of the trial. They all had a primary diagnosis of HSDD and the episode had to be present for at least 24 weeks. All women had a score of 15 or higher on the Female Sexual Distress Scale-Revised (FSDS-R) at the screening visit. The FSDS-R uses a 13-item questionnaire with scores from 0 to 52. They also had a score of 0 or 1 on Item #2 of the Sexual Interest and Desire Instrument-Female(SIDI-F). On the SIDI-F scoring is from 0= dissatisfied to 5 = very satisfied. Item #2 for SIDI-F simply asks "How satisfied are you with the sexual aspect of your relationship with your partner?" There were other criteria but these were the main inclusion criteria.

CLINICAL TRIAL DRUGS

For the three randomized placebo controlled pivotal trials, different drug doses were used. Study 511.71 subjects were randomized to one of

- Placebo
- Flibanserin 50mg qhs (at night)
- Flibanserin 100mg qhs

Study 511.75 subjects were randomized to one of

- Placebo
- Flibanserin 25mg bid
- Flibanserin 50mg bid
- Flibanserin 100mg qhs

The highest doses in Study 511.75 was accomplished by first placing subjects on 50mg qhs for 14 days and then up-titrating to the final doses of wither 50mg bid or 100mg qhs.

Study 511.147 subjects were randomized to either

- Placebo or
- Flibanserin 100mg qhs

FEMALE SEXUAL FUNCTION INDEX QUESTIONNAIRE
You can view the Female Sexual Function Index questionnaire at www.fsfiquestionnaire.com and score yourself.

Table 2. Female Sexual Function Index

Domain	Questions	Score Range	Factor	Minimum Score	Maximum Score	Your Score
Desire	1,2	1-5	0.6	1.2	6.0	
Arousal	3,4,5,6	0-5	0.3	0	6.0	
Lubrication	7,8,9,10	0-5	0.3	0	6.0	
Orgasm	11,12,13	0-5	0.4	0	6.0	
Satisfaction	14,15,16	0 or (1)-5	0.4	0.8	6.0	
Pain	17,18,19	0-5	0.4	0	6.0	
				2.0	36	
		Total				

Source: www.fsfiquestionnaire.com. Rosen et al 2000. Add up your scores. ≤ 26.55 = Female Sexual Dysfunction.

SEXUAL DISTRESS SCALE-REVISED FSDS-R
Table 3. Female Sexual Distress Scale
Scale: 0= Never; 1= Rarely; 2= Occasionally; 3= Frequently; 4= Always

	Question	Score	You
1	Distressed about your sex life?	1 2 3 4 5	
2	Unhappy about your sex life?	1 2 3 4 5	
3	Guilty about your sexual difficulties?	1 2 3 4 5	
4	Frustrated by your sexual problems?	1 2 3 4 5	
5	Stressed about sex?	1 2 3 4 5	
6	Inferior because of sexual problems?	1 2 3 4 5	
7	Worried about sex?	1 2 3 4 5	
8	Sexually inadequate?	1 2 3 4 5	
9	Regrets about your sexuality?	1 2 3 4 5	
10	Embarrassed about sexual problems?	1 2 3 4 5	
11	Dissatisfied with your sex life?	1 2 3 4 5	
12	Angry about your sex life?	1 2 3 4 5	
13	Bothered by low sexual desire?	1 2 3 4 5	
		Total	

Female Sexual Distress if score greater than 11.
Source: www.trihealth.com

86

Chapter 12

THE PINK TRIAL ENDPOINTS

PRIMARY AND SECONDARY ENDPOINTS

A total of three endpoints, two primary and one secondary, were chosen for the study trials. The two co-primary endpoints were satisfying sexual events (SSEs) and sexual desire. SSEs were measured by asking the subjects four questions. The first question asked if the subject had sex in the last 24 hours or more. If the answer was yes, then in addition to stating the day the sexual activity occurred, the subject was expected to state how many times she had sex, if the sex was satisfying and whether she had an orgasm with yes and no responses. The answers were recorded in an electronic eDiary or by memory recall. The very first eDiary entry asked about the previous 24 hours. Patients were given 7 days to recall the SSE in Study 511.147 and three days in Studies 511.71 and 511.75.

Sexual Desire was evaluated using the Female Sexual Function Index–Sexual Desire (FSFI-SD). This is a self-reporting questionnaire developed for use in women with hypoactive sexual desire disorder. It consists of 19 items in six domains

(Rosen et al., 2000). A 4-week recall version of the FSFI-SD was used in Study 511.147 meaning patients were asked to reflect back over the previous 28 days to answer the items in the questionnaire. Only the first two questions were employed as primary end points in final Study 511.147. These same two questions were used as secondary endpoints in the other two pivotal Studies 511.71 and 511.75. The first question focused on the frequency of interest and simply asked how often a patient felt sexual desire or interest. She was expected to rate this interest on a scale from 1(Almost never or never) to 5(Almost always or always). The second question asked the patient to rate their level of sexual desire from 1(Low or none) to 5(Very high).

The secondary endpoint, distress, was measured as the reported change in distress at week 24 from the patient's baseline distress. Distress was measured using the Functional Sexual Distress Scale-Revised (FSDS-R) 13-item questionnaire in Table 3. It was used to evaluate how women were affected by a given problem or challenge over the last 7 days.

EXTRAPOLATING ENDPOINT RESULTS

The two co-primary endpoints chosen for all three pivotal studies were Sexually Satisfying Events (SSE) and Sexual Desire. In Study 511.147 however, the sexual desire instrument was changed. In this study, that is Study 511.147, the more reliable daily e-diary was not used to assess sexual desire. Instead, the less reliable FSFI was used.

Participants were given three days to recall and record previous SSE's in Studies 511.71 and 511.75 and seven days to recall and record SSE's in Study 511.147. Subjects could enter data for differing number of days per four-week evaluation period. The daily average number of SSEs was then "standardized" using extrapolation to 28-day periods. This "standardization" is imperfect and can be misleading, particularly from a research and clinical perspective. We believe research reports as researchers always do an extremely thorough job. They have nothing to gain by misrepresenting their work or misleading the rest of the world. This "standardization" would however have caused any math professor to blush. Here's how it works. If a subject recorded SSEs 24 days during the 28-day period, Sprout officials "standardized" the data by a multiplier that boosts the number of SSEs.

It worked this way. If a person recorded 6 SSEs over 24 of the 28 days, Sprout made adjustments. Rather than record the actual 6 SSEs for that 28-day period, they "standardized" the 6 SSEs to arrive at a "Total Monthly Count of 8 SSEs as follows:

Total Monthly SSEs = 28 x (Total number of SSEs) ÷ (Total number of days recorded)

> Julia has been married for eighteen months and was diagnosed with HSDD 6 months after she married Jules. She is participating in Flibanserin Study 511.XX in California. Even when she feels aroused, she has an extremely busy schedule and is only available for SSEs on weekends (Saturdays

and Sundays) and gets one or two SSEs a month. She rests all day Saturday, leaving only Sunday morning. Since she started the Pink Pill, she has had one additional SSE in the twenty-eight days, making it two per month instead of just one. Julia is however frustrated because she thought the pill would turn things round. It seems to her that nothing much has changed. She is really frustrated and in anger refused to record the two SSEs for October. She did better with recording in the eDiary the following month and messed up again.

Statistically, Julia has had a 100% increase in SSEs. Clinically however, she is dissatisfied and has a right to feel so with SSEs only twice a month. She is available for SSEs for four weekends, 8 days during each 28-day period. She recorded in her eDiary daily for one week and had to recall from memory another uneventful week. Since she could not remember anything for the second week, she entered an additional SSE for that week just to be on the "safe side". She now has 2 SSEs for the fourteen-day period. In the third and fourth week that made up this final 28-day cycle, she had no other SSE but in her frustration forgot to record anything in the eDiary and admitted she could not remember. Her actual SSE for the entire month was 2. Based on Sprout's standardization method however, she would have a "standardized"

Total monthly count of SSEs =
$28 \times 2 \div 14 = 56 \div 14 = 4$ SSEs.

The actual number of SSEs is 2 but because of Julia's frustration and memory inaccuracies, the number of SSEs has now doubled. While there is no law against it, you don't over-inflate results to demonstrate an effect during clinical trials. You downplay your results so as to give greater credibility. If despite your downplay you still show significant results statistically and clinically, you probably have a winner. Obviously standardization simply means extrapolation. One wonders how many of the subjects had their SSEs extrapolated and mathematically analyzed and interpreted poorly. Another problem with the way the clinical trial data was analyzed was Sprout's method of handling missing efficacy data. If any results on SSEs desire or distress were missing, they would replace the missing data with the subject's previous response on their last visit. This was called estimation of missing data by using the last-observation-carried-forward (LOCF) method. Nice terminology but how dare anyone interpret what a subject's response should be for a particular month? What if last month's data was extrapolated using LOCF? How many LOCF's can you do and when does it become unethical? Would you want anyone to interpret your response as awesome if you weren't getting any real benefit from a clinical trial drug? According to the FDA records,

> "If less than 14 days of diary data were available for a given month, the most recent 28-day period with at least 14 days of available diary data was imputed for that month."

This LOCF method not only allowed unbridled data manipulation, it made the process appear technical scientific and justified. If the most recent 28-day period with at least 14 days of available diary data was three months ago, then the data will be manipulated to fit whatever was needed to create statistical significance for that month, and the next month and the next month. I'm not saying this is what Sprout did, but if that's what they did, what ethically or legally prevents them from doing so? According to Dr. Bert Spilker, if you are going to impute data, particularly safety and efficacy data, be sure to publish data analysis with and without imputation. That way anyone looking at the data analysis can see both and that the imputed data did not influence much of the results. While ethical and scientifically sound to provide data analysis with and without imputation for true comparisons, it's unclear whether Sprout provided data analysis without imputation to the FDA for comparison. This would be standard practice, is ethical, scientific and shows they operated in the best interests of patients, prescribers and any company seeking to purchase the rights to manufacture Pink.

There is no rule to date on how much data can be imputed. The real question is should you impute 50% of the required data set for one or more patients in a safety and efficacy trial? If you do, then shouldn't you also publish the data analysis without imputation of the data? That's why I think a real ethical dilemma exists regarding the statistical or clinical usefulness of data obtained in

Study 511.147, the final study for gaining FDA approval.

To fully appreciate the implications of this data imputing impunity, let's look at an example of satisfying sexual events for Julia over a 5-month period from September to January.

Table 4. Julia's Fictitious Data for SSEs

Month	Actual SSEs	Total days of eDiary entry per 28-day period
September	2	28
October	2	14
November	2	18
December	2	12
January	2	8

In all five months, Julia had 2 SSEs per month, a total of 10 SSEs, and she was unhappy about this. As a clinical trials subject however, here's what her new "standardized" scores would look like:

Table 5. Julia's Adjusted Data for SSEs

Month	Actual SSEs	Total eDiary entry days per 28-day period	Total Monthly SSEs After "Standardization"
September	2	28	N/A
October	2	14	4
November	2	18	3.1
December	2	12	4.6
January	2	8	7

Showing how Standardization/Imputation Impacts Reality

Julia in frustration did not record more than eight days in January for week 20. Yet the fewer days she recorded in the eDiary, the more SSEs were imputed and attributed to her. The data analyst interprets the 2 SSEs in January in light of the eight days recorded and arrives at a convenient 7 SSEs in January for Julia. What Sprout's data analyst should have done was to provide non-standardized data analysis of all the SSEs as well.

But what's the real story behind Julia's frustration and why 2 SSEs per month? She said she enjoyed sexual intercourse with her husband but believed it should occur only twice a month! Growing up as the youngest of six daughters, Julia's mother and later her older sisters when they got married, told her something fascinating about intimacy. "Sex must not occur more than twice a month if you want your husband to be a strong and good provider for the family" they all told her! No amount of "standardization" or medication can fix this paradigm. Only therapy could. She had sexual distress most of which stemmed from having a sex drive higher than the twice a month recommended to keep her husband strong. So even though she would only allow herself 2 SSEs per month without a therapist's intervention, she would be given 7 SSEs by imputation for January! This meant Pink has added 5 more SSEs to Julia's normal monthly SSEs even though in reality it didn't add anything. That is statistically significant isn't it? Every scientist knows that statistics can be used to convey any message the user wishes to.

Another more obvious problem with the interpretation of Study 511.147 data is the statistical analysis of recall for the 7-day and the 28-day recall of events by participants. According to the FDA BRUDAC records,

"For a subset of patients a 7-day recall version of the FSFI was administered at visit 8 (week 20) and visit 9(week 24). Because the primary endpoint was the FSFI using the standard 28-day recall period, the FSFI assessment for these patients at these visits that used the 7-day recall was considered missing, and LOCF using the previously available FSFI 28-day recall value was used in the primary analysis."

Why not just give the same subset of patients the 28-day FSFI questionnaire after they completed the 7-day recall version? Why did they have to use the LOCF in active patients that could have completed the 28-day questionnaire first? Did this subset of patients have a much sharper memory after completing the 7-day questionnaire and officials feared the outcome of such memory juggling? Could that be why they sent them "home" and imputed their data? It is obvious to anyone that recalling events that occurred within 7 days will be far more accurate than recalling events spread over 28 days. Yet Sprout convinced the FDA that the 7-day and 28-day recall periods were found to be almost exact with a 95% confidence interval and an 80-125% ratio. It's quite likely that the more accurate 7-day recall was unfavorable to the desired results as the less accurate 28-day recall period. They therefore cancelled the more accurate 7-day recall period FSFI results for that subset of patients above and treated it as missing data! They now used the LOCF to create newer more favorable data by duplicating a prior month's data! Why not just give the same subset of patients the 7-day and

28-day recall FSFI simultaneously at week 20 and week 24?

HOW MUCH CAN YOU REMEMBER?

According to an often quoted study on forgetting textbook materials, this is what you'll remember:

Table 6. Percentage recalled from memory

Days After	How much remembered
1	54%
7	35%
14	21%
21	18%
28	19%
63	17%

Source: www.faculty.bucks.edu.

This means you'll be able to recall roughly about three times more information on day 7 than you would on day 28. This table was obtained from the Bucks County Community College website at www.faculty.bucks.edu. I searched Google for "7-day memory recall versus same day". A May 2012 open archive www.sciencedirect.com article compared 7-day recall and daily diary reports of COPD symptoms in 101 adults with the disease. Patients were told to record their symptoms in a daily diary and also recall their symptoms after 7 days. Those allowed to recall their symptoms in 7 days overestimated their symptoms by 35 to 50 percent. That simply means a 7-day recall was over-inflated by about 50 percent compared to daily recall. What would happen in 28 days?

To help you understand how unreliable the 28-day FSFI instrument was for obtaining hard data, six patients from Flibanserin Study 511.144 patients were asked what type of recall they preferred for assessment of frequency and intensity of sexual desire. According to the FDA report, these 6 patients (40%) in Study 511.144 said they would have responded differently if asked about recalling in 24 hours or 7 days. It seemed they all preferred the daily or 7-day recall to the 28-day recall period used for the FSFI study. Would you prefer to recall vaguely what you could recall with greater clarity? I don't think so. Neither did the subjects. The bottom line is that a 28-day recall period is no good and confers no validity on the Pink Pill studies. Under scrutiny, the final study leading to approval of the Pink Pill, Study 511.147 used an unreliable instrument to achieve statistically significant outcomes using a 28-day recall. When the more reliable daily eDiary record was used in Studies 511.71 and 511.75, no statistically significant results were obtained.

Chapter 13

PINK TRIAL RESULTS

The next few paragraphs outline the clinical trial results for Flibanserin for the two co-primary and secondary endpoints as well as my interpretation of some of them. You should be able to draw your own independent conclusions after this. You can decide if you want to take the pill or if you will be comfortable recommending or prescribing it.

#1 SEXUALLY SATISFYING EVENTS (SSE)

For all three pivotal trials using flibanserin 100mg qhs (at night) or placebo in Studies 511.71, 511.75, and 511.147, there was a median increase of 1 SSE, 0.5 SSE and 0.5 SSE per month respectively from baseline at week 24. One additional sexual event a month is not that clinically significant. The risks of serious side effects seem to far outweigh this nearly intangible benefit. A physician without any secondary incentive should question his desire to write a prescription for the Pink Pill and weigh it carefully using a risk-benefit ratio. In the final analysis of SSEs, three studies were used, Studies 511.71, 511.75 and 51.147. Study 511.71 had 560 patients, Study 511.75 had 723 patients (excluding the 69 patients with data integrity-related issues from 2 sites) and Study 511.147 had 1021 patients. I will use the digits after the decimal for each study.

Table 7. Sexually Satisfying Events (SSE) Score from 3 Trials

	Study 71		Study 75		Study 147	
	F 100	P	F 100	P	F 100	P
# Patients	275	285	358	365	500	521
At Baseline	3.0	2.0	2.0	2.0	2.0	2.0
At Week 24*	4.0	2.8	3.0	2.8	4.0	3.0
Median Change	1.0	0.0*	1.0	0.5	1.0	0.5
Treatment diff	1		0.5		0.5	
P value	<0.05		<0.05		<0.05	

F 100 = Flibanserin 100mg; P = Placebo; diff= difference
Source: FDA Briefing Document Joint Meeting of BRUDAC and DSaRM Advisory Committee, June 4, 2015.
*. *Strange that Median Change for Placebo in Study 71 is 0 instead of 0.8*

PROBLEMS WITH STUDY 511.71

Some numbers just don't look right in Study 71. The SSE at baseline in the placebo group was 2.0 and at week 24 it had gone up to 2.8. That's a 40% increase from baseline and statistically that is significant. Yet Sprout claims, and as Table 7 suggests, that this 40% change by week 24, a classic placebo number, is a median change of zero. How can a difference of 40% be considered a median change of zero in the same patient population? Puzzling!

TREATMENT DIFFERENCE

This is the difference between the treatment group (Flibanserin 100mg at night) and the placebo group. Whenever a drug company states its claims about the usefulness of a drug, it usually does so by highlighting (1) the difference between their drug and another drug or (2) the difference between their drug and placebo. Since there is no drug for female sexual arousal with which Pink can be compared, the only option of comparison for Sprout is option (2), placebo comparison. At the end of 24 weeks Spout claims that flibanserin increases the SSEs in patients with FSIAD or HSDD by an additional 0.5 to 1.0 event per month. This claim is based on the treatment differences between Flibanesrin 100mg hs and placebo for all three studies, 511.71, 511.75 and 511.147. This treatment difference is obtained by subtracting the median changes obtained in the placebo group from the median changes obtained from the flibanserin group in each study.

For study 511.147 the treatment difference is
Median change for Pink – Median change for Placebo
1.0 – 0.5 = 0.5

For Study 511.75 the treatment difference is
Median change for Pink – Median change for Placebo
1.0 – 0.5 = 0.5

For Study 511.71 the treatment difference is
Median change for Pink – Median Change for Placebo
1.0 – 0.0 = 1.0

The placebo effect cannot be zero. Yet the treatment difference in study 511.71 is based on a median change of zero in the placebo group! This zero median change is responsible for the higher treatment difference between placebo group and Pink group in study 511.71 compared to the other two studies. This difference is the one used by Sprout to lay the claim that Pink adds one SSE per month. Can that claim really be without doubt? Giving the placebo group 0.0 instead of 0.4 skews

100

the efficacy results in favor of Pink. I'm not sure if this was an unintended error or my inability to properly interpret statistical data but a median change of zero in the placebo group is an unpardonable typo. What would the number be if instead of 0.0 an actual number such as 0.4 were plugged in?

#2 SEXUAL DESIRE RESULTS

As reported by the FDA, flibanserin failed to show any statistical difference compared to placebo when sexual desire was measured by the daily eDiary method. When sexual desire was then measured using the 28-day recall FSFI-D instrument, flibanserin showed a statistical improvement over placebo in increasing sexual desire from baseline. In Studies 71, 75, and 147, sexual desire increased by 0.9, 0.9, and 1.0 in the Pink group and by 0.5, 0.6 and 0.7 in the Placebo group in Studies 71, 75 and 147 respectively. While statistically significant, it isn't clinically significant.

Table 8. Sexual Desire Score by FSFI-Desire Domain

SEXUAL DESIRE (SD)	Study 71		Study 75		Study 147	
	F 100	P	F 100	P	F 100	P
# Patients	280	290	358	365	506	525
At Baseline	1.9	1.9	1.8	1.8	1.9	1.9
At Week 24	2.8	2.4	2.7	2.4	2.9	2.6
LS Mean Change	0.9	0.5	0.9	0.6	1.0	0.7
Treatment diff	0.3(0.2, 0.4)		0.4(0.2, 0.5)		0.3(0.2, 0.5)	
P value	<0.05		<0.05		<0.05	

F 100 = Flibanserin 100mg; P = Placebo; diff= difference
Source: FDA Briefing Document Joint Meeting of BRUDAC and DSaRM Advisory Committee, June 4, 2015

#3 DISTRESS RESULTS

The third parameter, distress was a secondary endpoint. All three pivotal studies 511.71, 511.75 and 511.147 showed a statistically significant effect with flibanserin on sexual distress compared with placebo. This however does not translate into clinical significance. But even here, there are questions regarding the data presented to the FDA.

Table 9. Summary Results for Distress (Using FSDS-R Q13)

	Study 71		Study 75		Study 147	
	F 100	P	F 100	P	F 100	P
# Patients	280	289	389	380	506	525
At Baseline	3.2	3.2	3.3	3.2	3.4	3.4
At Week 24	2.8	2.4	2.7	2.4	2.9	2.6
LS Mean Change	0.9	0.5	0.9	0.6	1.0	0.7
Treatment Diff.	-0.3(-0.4, -0.1)		-0.4(-0.5, -0.2)		-0.3(-0.4, -0.1)	
P value	<0.05		<0.05		<0.05	

F 100 = Flibanserin 100mg; P = Placebo; diff= difference
Source: FDA Briefing Document Joint Meeting of BRUDAC and DSaRM Advisory Committee, June 4, 2015

QUESTIONABLE RESULTS AT WEEK 24!

If you look carefully at Table 8 (Sexual Desire) and Table 9, the one for distress above, you might not immediately notice a strange phenomenon for the results at week 24. Both tables are reporting two different parameters, two different baselines and two different endpoints. Table 8 looks at Sexual Desire at baseline and at the end of 24 weeks. Table 9 looks at Distress at baseline and at the week 24. Do you notice anything unusually familiar about week 24 in both tables? Look again.

102

Placed side by side, the baseline scores for Sexual Desire in the Flibanserin and Placebo groups are 1.9,1.9; 1.8,1.8 and 1.9,1.9 for Studies 71, 75 and 147 respectively. At week 24 these numbers have increased from their baseline to 2.8,2.4; 2.7,2.4 and 2.9,2.6 respectively for Flibanserin and Placebo groups.

The baseline Distress levels in the Flibanserin and Placebo group were 3.2,3.2; 3.3,3.2 and 3.4,3.4 for Studies 71, 75 and 147 respectively. At week 24 as expected for an FDA-approved drug, the numbers for distress had decreased to 2.8,2.4; 2.7,2.4 and 2.9,2.6 respectively for Flibanserin and Placebo groups. Some things really struck me as odd here. The three pairs of numbers at week 24 for Sexual Desire are identical to the three pairs of numbers for Distress at week 24. Secondly, in the Flibanserin group of study 71, the difference between baseline distress of 3.2 and 2.8 at week 24 cannot be greater than 0.4? Yet it is 0.9. The LS mean changes in both tables are identical despite having different baseline numbers. What a coincidence!

Table 10. Desire vs. Distress Scores at Baseline and Week 24

	Study 71		Study 75		Study 147	
SEXUAL DESIRE (SD)	F 280	P 290	F 358	P 365	F 506	P 525
At Baseline	1.9	1.9	1.8	1.8	1.9	1.9
At Week 24**	2.8	2.4	2.7	2.4	2.9	2.6
LS Mean Change	0.9	0.5	0.9	0.6	1.0	0.7
DISTRESS	Study 71		Study 75		Study 147	
	F 280	P 289	F 358	P 365	F 506	P 525
At Baseline	3.2	3.2	3.3	3.2	3.4	3.4
At Week 24	2.8	2.4	2.7	2.4	2.9	2.6
LS Mean Change?						

Below is an even much simpler table showing desire and distress scores at baseline and at Week 24.

Table 11. Desire and Distress Scores

		Study 71		Study 75		Study 147	
		F	P	F	P	F	P
Desire	Baseline	1.9	1.9	1.8	1.8	1.9	1.9
Score	Week 24*	2.8	2.4	2.7	2.4	2.9	2.6
Distress	Week 24**	2.8	2.4	2.7	2.4	2.9	2.6
Score	Baseline	3.2	3.2	3.3	3.2	3.4	3.4

F= Flibanserin 100mg hs; P = Placebo */** duplicated data?

Table 10 compresses actual data from the two table summaries of Sexual Desire (Table 8) and Distress (Table 9) from page 31 of the BRUDAC/DSaRM June 4, 2015 *FDA Briefing Document*. Table 11 further compresses this data so you can see the duplicate numbers for Sexual Desire and Distress at week 24. This should raise several questions about the duplication of data that appears in week 24.

First, what is the probability that both number pairs for sexual desire and distress would be identical for all three studies at week 24? Secondly, what should be the LS Mean Change values for distress? If you never used to do your math homework when you were younger, you should have fun figuring out the LS Mean Change for Distress for all three studies by filling in the empty boxes in table 10 with a pencil. The LS Mean Change is simply the difference between the values at Baseline and at Week 24. Thirdly, were the numbers for Distress in week 24 accidentally cut and paste from the *Sexual Desire* table or are these the actual Distress data? If the numbers were accidentally placed from Sexual Desire data, then where is the actual Distress data? If the LS Mean Change numbers for Distress at week 24 are based on the actual data collected and not mistakenly placed, then it means that placebo reduced distress far more than flibanserin. The lower distress numbers for placebo at week 24 meant that placebo reduced distress to a greater extent than Pink. Is that what Sprout was really trying to communicate? You be the judge.

I have devoted the greater part of my professional life over the last twenty years to writing, teaching and helping couples understand how to build their marriages. In that time I have seen so much unnecessary sexual starvation as a cause of many marital woes. My hope for this pill was with mixed excitement and curiosity but that has led to a more thorough evaluation of the pink pill. Frankly, even if everyone didn't want to take the pill and it had excellent data behind it, I would have gathered support for it without the company having to pay a dime to me for advertising. Not only that, I would be one of the foremost prescribers due to the nature of the people I counsel and consult. In other words, Sprout Pharmaceuticals could never have had a stronger advocate for their pink pill if it had all the science behind it. As a physician, public speaker, ordained minister and an expert on the medical complications of divorce and marriage building, they couldn't have asked for more in an advocate for the pill.

The summarized distress data with the sexual desire date in week 24 seem to be more than a perfect coincidence.

There is one unusual indication for flibanserin based on the studies I might suggest: shy women who want to hide their expression of their erotic self behind the Pink Pill. They can blame it on the pink pill. But even in such women, the undesirable side effects of flibanserin still outweigh its benefits. The degree of data "standardization" and the dangerous side effects with the potentially catastrophic consequences make this a drug one should probably not prescribe until more convincing evidence and post-marketing trials reveal a greater benefit and safety profile. Hopefully, this would happen and we will all sigh a relief and welcome the Pink Pill to the therapeutic Hall of Fame for the 21st Century!

Chapter 14

SIDE EFFECTS OF FLIBANSERIN

Remember when letters where tossed back and forth between the FDA and the owners of Pink in earlier chapters? The biggest concern the FDA had was with the safety profiles demonstrated and the need for greater clarification on safety issues. Flibanserin causes central nervous system effects leading to fatigue, somnolence and sedation. If taken late at night, it can lead to motor impairment the next day because of its long roughly 12-hour half-life. So if you take the Pink Pill at 10pm for example, you may still be experiencing difficulty with alertness in the morning about 10am. The sedative effects of the 100mg flibanserin dose was maximal about two hours after oral administration and was mostly reversed by 6 hours, the study trials reported.

Flibanserin was reported as having a narrow safety margin with 250mg being the maximally tolerated dose. One of the 36 patients receiving 250mg flibanserin fell and dislocated the right shoulder on the third day after treatment during the washout period between doses! One of the 35 patients receiving the 200mg dose, (Subject #1048), experienced syncope, (fainting spell) one hour after receiving the drug. These are side effects that could lead to accidental injury and deaths. There are medico-legal issues beyond the scope of this book that could arise when a physician prescribes the pink pill to a woman who denies alcohol use but goes on to have a fatal accident after using alcohol. The half-life of the drug guarantees that long after the alcohol levels have diminished significantly, the flibanserin levels measured in the blood could still implicate the prescriber. A few years ago, a 33-year old police officer died following a threesome with two people (none of them his wife) at a hotel in Atlanta, Georgia. Even though sudden coital death is common and well described in the medical literature, the patient's family sued the cardiologist for not warning him to "avoid a threesome" and won! So while on flibanserin, any accident and loss of life, limb or property may be blamed on the prescribing physician and not the patient.

ALCOHOL AND FLIBANSERIN

Pink should not be taken with alcohol. Since flibanserin must be taken daily without any suggestions by its manufacturers of a drug holiday, it means you should never drink while on the pink pill. Is that something the average woman is willing to accept or is it something she will try to circumvent by sipping just a little bit of wine every now and then? Alcohol use is common in settings preceding sexual activity and the combination of alcohol and flibanserin increases the likelihood of severe hypotension and syncope. Sprout had difficulty recruiting female patients for their flibanserin-alcohol. Probably aware of the potential adverse effects, most women could not be recruited for the flibanserin-alcohol trials requested by the

FDA. As a result, 23 of the 25 subjects tested for the effect of alcohol on flibanserin were men. This is a drug safety issue and yet the drug was approved for use in a patient population whose majority could not be tested for the drug-alcohol interaction before approval! Did that really bypass the FDA's scrutiny? As a woman, would you take a pill meant for women but whose drug-alcohol interactions were checked in only 8% of women and 92% of men? What could be more sexist on Sprout's part than that? Significant drops in systolic and diastolic blood pressures were reported resulting in dizziness, orthostatic hypotension and syncope. Systolic drops in blood pressure ranged between 27 and 57 mm Hg and diastolic blood pressure drops ranged between 10 and 48mm Hg. Many of these patients were in their 20's and 30's.

There was only one death in a subject in Study 511.74 who received placebo. She died in a plane crash on day 19 of the double-blind period. One can only presume she wasn't the pilot. None of the adverse effects of depression were serious or statistically significant in the placebo and pink groups.

WHY YOU SHOULD BE CONCERNED

My major concerns about the pink pill Addyi are its poorly demonstrated efficacy, poorly addressed adverse effects, amount of data manipulation during the clinical trials and the potential but undisclosed long-term central nervous system (CNS) and psychiatric effects.

EFFECTIVENESS CONCERNS

In the real world patients don't care about statistics, they just want results. Patients who take the pink pill daily have a chance to add one more SSE per month. What about those who miss two, three or even a week's dose? Do they have a chance? Will one more sexual encounter per month be enough for a sex-starved marriage? In real life in a real marriage, what is half a sexually satisfying event? You must be kidding. Taking a pill for thirty days just to get one additional sexual encounter or half a sexual encounter (whatever that means) is not an indication of effectiveness. In my opinion it would have to provide at least one additional sexual encounter per week or at least two to three additional SSEs per month to be of any significant clinical value. As a husband, minister, marriage builder, physician, potential prescriber of Addyi and divorce prevention expert married for over 18 years, I think these are reasonable demands placed on the pink pill. Comparing Viagra with Addyi might be like comparing apples and oranges, but Viagra delivers the same day while Addyi delivers only one more event in 28 days at best and only after "standardization".

COST CONCERNS

My second concern is the cost-effectiveness of a daily pill. Spending that much money to get only one additional sexual encounter a month is not likely to improve a sex starved marriage. If you need four to six satisfying sexual encounters a month to get your marriage where it needs to be, will Pink be able to get you there and save your marriage? Probably not! A mathematical approach to evaluating the effectiveness of Pink as well as a clinical one should help you grasp how much waste is going to occur with the use of this drug. Suppose you take an antihypertensive pill to lower your blood pressure. You expect that everyday you take the pill you will get an effective lowering of your blood pressure. You wouldn't expect to take the pill for thirty days and have your blood pressure lowered just one out of thirty days would you? If that happens with your blood pressure pill your doctor will increase the dose or change the drug. Well you might protest and say this is comparing apples and oranges. Okay, I'll admit it is. So if you are a man and you take Viagra® or Cialis®, won't you expect an effect the same day and within a few hours? You would if you were getting your money's worth. If you take a pill and you're getting an effect only one out of thirty days, you should know you're not getting your money's worth. That drug has an efficacy of 1/30 multiplied by 100% or 3.3%. Would you ask for a refund? Bet you probably would!

SIDE EFFECTS CONCERNS

My third concern is that it is unclear how much attempt was made to understand and address the reason for the side effects. As a clinician with significant emergency medicine and critical care experience who has cared for head injury patients following syncope, I would want to know a few things that were done when the clinical trials subjects fainted. For example, were these patients well hydrated before treatment? Did they have an EKG done right after fainting and was this normal? Who read the EKG? Was there prolongation of the QT interval on the EKG? Should some patients get an EKG before starting flibanserin? While a coronary event is unlikely, were cardiac enzymes checked? Should patients drink a glass or three of water before taking Pink to mitigate the orthostatic hypotension that could develop later? The trials did not answer any of these questions.

STATISTICAL DATA CONCERNS
Fourthly and as you can see, too much data extrapolation, imputing, standardization occurred in spite of which the Pink pill did not produce convincing clinical evidence of superiority over placebo overall. Look at Tables 8,9,10 and 11.

PSYCHIATRY-RELATED CONCERNS
My final concern is about the potential adverse psychiatric effects of flibanserin unmentioned in the trials. Classifying Pink along with Trazodone is a fair one. This places it squarely in the category of an antidepressant. This however means its efficacy, like that of other antidepressants, should now be in question. Antidepressants have a bad reputation for not having any truly high impact on depressed patients. Except in the most severely depressed patients, antidepressants have little positive impact. According to Dr. Irving Kirsch, British psychologist and author of *The Emperor's New Drugs: Exploding The Antidepressant Myth*, the antidepressants Effexor, Paxil, Prozac, Effexor and Serzone were drugs with very little specific

112

therapeutic benefit but with serious side effects. Does that ring a bell? Dr. Kirsch obtained all the clinical trial data he could on antidepressants in England and went as far as invoking the *Freedom of Information Act* to obtain undisclosed clinical trial data on antidepressants in the United States. The results were impressive and showed that close to 40% of clinical trial data were withheld. As a result of Dr. Kirsch's work, Britain's National Institute of Health and Clinical Excellence (NICE), the organization that draws up clinical treatment guidelines for the United Kingdom's National Health Service (NHS), has acknowledged that antidepressants do not provide any clinically significant benefit to most depressed patients. I believe the effect of flibanserin is mostly placebo and not any real drug effect. The clinical trial evidence itself proves this to be so at this point. Perhaps post-marketing surveys will reveal a better performance picture.

PART 3
RELATIONSHIPS

"The Swedish study consisted of 989 men born ten years apart, in 1913 and 1923 respectively, and followed for 10 years, from 1973 to 1982. Among the 60-year olds, 25 percent of those who lived alone died compared with 7 percent of those living with four or more persons. Similarly amongst the 50-year olds, 13 percent of those who lived alone died compared with 3 percent of those living with four or more persons. It appears that living alone almost quadruples the risk of dying and one antidote to such death is to live with four or more people." (Welin et al, 1985).

Above excerpt from *Divorce Medicine: How Divorce and Toxic Relationships Affect Your Health*. 2015.

Chapter 15

MARITAL SEX IS DIFFERENT

Sex and marital intimacy are the first two things the Bible mentions in describing the relationship between a man and a woman. Sex is a grand divine design associated with grand benefits and producing grand results. Sex induces or forces the human race to perpetuate, communicate, accommodate, tolerate and celebrate each other and enjoy an ecstasy that could sometimes be described as out of this world. That sex is good is an understatement, it is a theme that should ring from the pulpit of every church, mosque and synagogue. Taking Eve out of Adam's rib is a sign that God wants permanence in the closeness between husband and wife. It would enable the man and his wife to resonate with each other's heartbeat in harmony, unity, synchrony and synergy. Declaring and celebrating this harmony and unity with a continually deepening intimacy through sex is boldly proclaimed in the second chapter of the Bible:

Therefore shall a man leave his father and his mother, and shall cleave unto his wife: and they two shall be one flesh. And they were both naked, the man and his wife, and were not ashamed. Genesis 2:24-45

Sex in the right context makes you happier, healthier, more focused, productive and calmer. Your creative capacity is multiplied many times over. You're more likely to be wealthier if your sex life in your marriage is rich. Outside of marriage, sex is a drug with unpredictable effects. It may, like alcohol, lead to intoxication, addiction and liver cirrhosis. It can behave like the cigarette you smoked hoping to relax but ends up causing emphysema or cancer of the throat or lungs. Many of those I knew decades ago who had "rich" sex lives even though they were single at the time don't have it richly anymore. It's those who seemed to have nothing to offer then that are enjoying most of what marital sex has to offer today. Ever watch the TV series *Sex and The City*? Notice how these single women live such empty tortured superficial meaningless lives without contributing much to their community? All they do is forage the male pool for sex while ignoring the possibility of getting infected with HIV!

Good sex can make a bad marriage tolerable and a good one great. No sex can make even good marriages intolerable. Every married couple must learn what stimulates and excites their partner sexually and what turns them off. Smells, touch, parts of speech and sounds can all be optimized for a healthy sex life. If you're married and you say you don't care, you're probably suffering the consequences of ignorance and lack of adequate sexual intimacy already. You have the power to change this. Find time to discuss each other's needs in a private place. This might save you both hours of therapy or a more expensive divorce later.

Remember how I mentioned that women have a piece of heaven inside them? That piece must be shared between husbands and wives to experience heaven on earth in their marriage. You can and you should. No matter how spiritual you are about sex, there is no doctrine about satisfying your partner. You just do it. You do everything you can to satisfy each other and leave your psychological past alone. Don't bring that past into your bedroom except you have an imaginary friend who sleeps with you without your husband's knowledge. If that is the case you need an exorcism not a therapist or best-selling book.

If you are religious, know that your willingness and actual meeting of your spouse's natural and divinely placed sexual needs is faithfulness and godliness. If you're not sure about this, check First Corinthians 7:3-5 and Hebrews 13:4. I am aware that many people claiming to follow the Bible's instructions do not read the Bible regularly or understand what to do after reading. But there are many others who read it but refuse to practice what they understand. You may be observing or listening to such misleading individuals and trust that they are feeding you with the right information. You however have a responsibility to study on your own and let common sense do some of the work for you. You must be faithful with the gift of your sexuality and the only place to be truly faithful with this precious gift is in your marriage, not as the town bicycle or Casanova. Unfaithfulness with the gift of your sexuality in your marriage can take many forms. Withholding sex, ignoring your partner's physical needs, failing to study and learn what would make your partner enjoy the pleasure of this gift in a way that deepens your love for each other, or using sex as a weapon of manipulation are all examples of such unfaithfulness. They may lead to some eternal consequences that are not fit for the pages of this book. If good sex heals the wounds of the psyche but you refuse to have sex with your husband or wife because you prefer your grudge to your marriage, that's a combination of ignorance and insanity. You don't have to be the cause of your spouse's wounded psyche but through sexual intimacy you can be the source of their healing. I guarantee you that if you choose insanity there are no insane people in heaven.

Behavioral scientists have told us over and again that there are so many advantages to healthy sexual intimacy between married couples. If we wait patiently for the right time, we will avoid most of the 870,000 pregnancies occurring each year among females between the ages of 15 and 19 in the US alone. Many of these young girls can't even feed themselves. Similarly, about 3 million cases of sexually transmitted diseases (STDs) are diagnosed annually in those aged 10-19. An article published in the *Journal of the American Medical Association* in 1999 put the number of women with sexual problems at 43%. That's an epidemic. While pleasure seems to be the driving force behind sex before marriage, there are medical and psychological consequences associated with sex outside of marriage. These include post-traumatic stress disorder (PTSD), Posttraumatic Embitterment Disorder (PTED), depression, unwanted pregnancy, abortion, pelvic inflammatory disease, infertility, poverty and a host of other undiagnosed psychological problems. A woman so comfortable with her sexuality that she uses it to lure men for her own personal comfort before marriage will likely continue to do so after marriage. She will have developed a bad habit based on the idea that sex is meant just for her comfort. She is unlikely to suddenly become a good wife who enjoys and deepens her love for her husband through sexual intimacy in the marriage. If she marries, she is more likely to feel empty and caged in the marriage. This is partly because sex, the crowning celebration of her love for her husband, has been used for something less noble before she married. She has learnt at the deepest seat of her soul that sex is only for her pleasure. She may feel as if she is in a psychiatric ward and be constantly seeking a way or excuse to escape from the marriage. If she is the confident accomplished type, she may gather friends around her to constantly sully her husband's dignity and reputation. Such women can go on with their negative ranting even when the man hasn't done anything wrong or worthy of character assassination. All she wants is a divorce and a way of convincing herself her husband is a bad man to justify the divorce. Such women are very good at looking for faults in their husbands and not the good in them. She may in extreme instances set him up with a friend or pay a prostitute just to get him to commit an act that would justify the divorce. You may think this is crazy, but for those who desperately want to divorce a good spouse, this is the least of things such a woman can attempt.

For such a woman, since marital intimacy seems impossible, any sin is the unforgiveable sin. All she's looking for is a way out of the grave called marriage, a grave she created long before she married. She'll scheme plot and plan the downfall of her own husband and marriage in order to get out of the mess she created through misuse of sex years earlier. Anything the man does, and he is out of her life, anything. She is at risk of developing FSIAD and bouts of depression and anger tantrums. The online edition of the November 12, 2012 *New York Daily News* reported the story of a 41-year old British woman who was divorcing her husband because he would not comply with the "instructions" from E.L James' *Fifty Shades of Grey*.

More Pain Than Money or Beauty Can Buy?

You'll find many such successful beautiful women in this category who at a glance appear to have everything together until they share their woes with you. Many of them can be found in the front rows of Mega-churches around the country with more than enough money to spend for the rest of their lives. They are seeking healing for their wounded souls and are faithful churchgoers. They sponsor church events but because the primary source of their wounded souls remains uncovered and therefore unaddressed, they themselves remain empty within. Hold such a woman's hands or touch her on the shoulder and look straight into her eyes, and you'll see her "success countenance and beauty" melt before your eyes. With tears running down her cheeks, you'll know there is more pain than money or beauty can buy. They bruised their souls because they had the freedom to pursue any type of sensual pleasure. Now their pain is hiding under mascara, designer clothing and Gucci bags or the usual glass of wine. False freedom has left its wounds and these are not battle wounds one can be proud of. They thought they were free to do anything but now they need someone to set them free. They've been searching for freedom but it constantly eludes them. They need a miracle. They need spiritual help and by God they will find it when they humble themselves, pray and ask God for forgiveness and turn from their old ways of satisfying the desires of the temporal flesh.

Healing Past Sexual Wounds of The Soul

These women need to forgive themselves and renounce their past in a way that only a Christian pastor can help them accomplish. After attending different churches and teaching and speaking around the world, I have developed a rudimentary classification for the different types of pastors and the different types of churches with respect to helping the wounded to heal. So for this type of woman, I would recommend she talk to a pastor of a Christian congregation with less than 200 people where the Bible is taught soundly without any undue regard for political correctness or sensationalism. It should be a place where the spiritual and emotional challenges of life are addressed in a balanced practical biblical manner: a place where the possibility of being filled with the power of the Holy Spirit is unashamedly preached regularly. She should also inquire about the possibility of deliverance, praying and fasting, recovery of her virtues lost through past sexual encounters. She can dedicate or rededicate her life completely to God and start afresh. This should be accompanied subsequently by appropriate and adequate follow up. This should be an in-depth follow-up by someone experienced with spiritual matters, the need for deliverance as well as strange sexual encounters that may occur while asleep or dreaming. This can be accomplished by seeing a well-grounded Christian friend, pastor or marriage therapist. Male or female, the affected individual should get involved with a healthy spiritual growth group, preferably one with a mix of different ages. I'm sure my critics are saying "what?" but who cares? Whom the Son sets free is free indeed! Only God can set such an individual free! Not Pink and not any pill.

If the Son therefore shall make you free,
ye shall be free indeed. John 8:36

There are also men who live "rich and fulfilling" sex lives of playboys before marriage. The more women they have slept with before marriage, the more insensitive and disoriented they may become about meeting a woman's real needs. When such men eventually marry, their lives seem to be a constant corrosive battlefield. The people you sleep with take something from you that may never be retrieved without a miracle. A beautiful young lady in her early thirties I pastored years ago brought in a young man to the church one Sunday morning. She was still dating a slightly older man than she was. I wanted to know who was the hunter and who, the hunted. It turned out that the young man was twenty and had dropped out of college because of his "love". The lady was thirty-five and you can decide who the predator was. She immediately told me she specialized in seducing men and that she sees any man she gets into her bed as the weaker vessel! Surprised at this paradigm shift of the new millennium, I decided to find out "how strong" she was by how many men she had "captured". She had sampled over fifty men at that point, roughly 1.5 men for every year of her life! We moved on to another subject when she lost count. She would need the same prescription above and probably a miracle. She may appear normal in church but if she ever marries, all the missing pieces of herself she shared with more than fifty men will turn her marriage into a battlefield. She will need deliverance and sexual rehabilitation.

Chapter 16

SEXUAL DESENSITIZATION

There are a host of experiences and factors in a woman's life that may increase her likelihood of developing FSIAD. Some of these factors apply equally to men as they do to women. I call these the CPR of sexual desensitization. C is for cohabitation, P is for pornography, promiscuity and perversion and R is for rape.

Sexual Desensitization Through Rape

Rape can lead to sexual desensitization and much later, FSIAD. While the frigidity resulting from rape may be assumed, predicted or at least understood, when there has been rape, no one even thinks of the possibility of cohabitation leading to any future sexual problems such as FSIAD. Rape may operate through a combination of trauma, fear and posttraumatic stress and desensitize a woman to her own normal sexual needs. A caring sensitive woman can shut down completely from sexual intimacy as a result of rape. Married women that avoid sex and make up either excuses or excess activities just to avoid sexual intimacy in their marriage should be asked if they had experienced sexual violation before the marriage. Those without any known mental illness have probably encountered rape in their early childhood or adult years. This is a very delicate issue as the woman freezes in time and needs gentleness and care and perhaps counseling. Regardless of whatever wounds the rape had caused, any woman that marries after rape is admitting that she needs intimacy and will also willingly give it. She must also recognize that she doesn't have to shut down in the marriage completely; she can heal and it will only be by choice. She will heal faster if she is sexually, emotionally and physically available to her husband. That way her husband provides strength and safety that allows her wounds to heal and her femininity to blossom. In the words of Sheila Kelly in her TED Talk

"The masculinity is for protecting the feminine so that the feminine can blossom and radiate and glow and in turn transform everything it touches."
- Let's Get Naked: Sheila Kelly TEDx Dec 18,2012

A female rape victim's goal, if she marries with good intentions, is to share herself so she can heal completely. She should get stronger if she marries a caring husband. If she is not getting stronger and more comfortable and has married a caring husband, then she is probably not opening up to the man or meeting his most intimate needs. That would be a one-sided marriage in which she gets all the benefits she desires; safety, strength, comfort, companionship and probably more but fails to give the man what he needs. Nothing could be more selfish. This will create an unhealthy imbalance in the relationship. If it persists, the man may change completely either after gentle nudging or even counseling. If she opens up by choice or unconsciously and meets those needs, she will have a better man and she herself will heal completely. If she doesn't open up and therefore fails to mature enough to meet the man's needs, she may end up with a bitter man. The needs she doesn't have to meet today may be needs she better not fail to meet tomorrow. The man is not made of steel but flesh as some women presume. He has needs and ignoring them will bring out the worst in him. I have seen and heard and then investigated different types of accusations by wives who ignore all the primary needs of their husbands. Many later admitted to rape either of themselves or someone close enough to them that they were hurt almost just as much as the rape victim. A rape victim may not intentionally ignore their partner's needs. It should however be clear that if you're getting what you need in a marriage, you're getting those things from another human being whose needs must also be met by you. So stop playing victim, get help and understand the needs of your partner. Be humble, mature and responsible enough to meet these needs of the other person.

If you're a rape victim, determine before marriage if you will meet your spouse's most important needs before plunging blindly into marriage. Don't use the marriage to punish the man who raped you before you met your husband. If a man finds you attractive enough to want to marry you, his number one reason for that marriage is to canoodle! It's not to visit the malls or write "Mr. & Mrs." on some stationery or mailbox. Similarly, if you are a man that wants to marry a woman, ask yourself if you're ready to meet the woman's deepest needs. Most men do not connect deeply with their emotions enough to meet the woman's deepest longings but they can learn if they are willing. The man who presumes he knows everything is not worth marrying if the woman doesn't want to suffer emotionally.

Here, according to Willard Harley, author of *His Needs, Her Needs,* are the most important needs you must meet if you want to stay married. If for some reason, you've been able to avoid meeting those needs, then it's time for change. You can't get away with neglecting the other person's needs forever; your sins will eventually find you out!

Top 5 Needs of Husbands Ranked by Importance
1. Sexual fulfillment
2. Recreational companionship
3. Attractive spouse
4. Domestic support
5. Admiration

Wife's Top 5 Needs Ranked by Importance
1. Affection
2. Conversation
3. Honesty and Openness
4. Financial support
5. Family Commitment.

So if you're a female rape victim, it'll be pointless for you to marry a man if you have no intention of meeting his most important needs. If you don't want to meet the man's sexual needs getting married is a foolish option. You'd be fooling yourself by getting married if you don't get past the trauma because while you may find security and comfort by marrying a good man, you will not find fulfillment. Not everyone can get past their trauma, but most can and those who don't often have made that choice. If you can't get past the trauma, don't marry. A woman that insists on marrying despite refusing to get help and get past the trauma may turn her husband into her own monster, particularly if the man is meeting her own important needs. Such husbands are often painted to the world as monsters and unfortunately the world isn't yet tired of hearing about such husbands. You might be thinking, "I don't meet my husband's sexual needs but I don't paint him as a monster. Perhaps that's because there can only be one monster in the marriage where needs are neglected and if you admit he is not the monster, then it's obvious who is. Living the life of a victim is a choice and the penalties are usually a lack of joy, fulfillment, unity, synergy and harmony. FSIAD remains a part of such relationships and both need to open up and grow. If the woman insists on playing the victim she will eventually involute, growing inward and becoming cancerously self-centered. She may gradually develop bodily symptoms and perhaps even physical illnesses that cannot be explained based on her age, health or family history.

Rape victims can heal. They heal faster and deeper by giving and receiving love and getting therapy. Sometimes they may not need therapy. Most men won't last if their physical and emotional needs are neglected forever in a marriage. Their needs have to be met somehow. A rape victim may remain unyielding to intimacy and loving affection. She may refuse to receive the two top women's needs above from a loving husband and if she does, is unlikely to meet the man's top needs. I know a few Christian women who have all they need in a man but still refuse to change and give the man what he needs. That man becomes the victim eventually. If the woman reveals the rape event to the man before they marry, he isn't expecting his wife to be frigid and he wants to love her back to wholeness. She still has a responsibility to meet the husband's physical needs. Even if the man is a crisis counselor dealing with rape victims regularly, he can't be starved sexually forever in his own marriage. A rape victim may shrivel away from physical contact and emotional intimacy. Even then the woman is obligated to meet the expected needs of her husband as she expects hers to be met. Otherwise why marry?

Sexual Desensitization Through Cohabitation

Cohabitation also contributes to FSIAD through desensitization. It is doubtful if cohabiting singles are aware that a woman could develop FSIAD as a consequence of cohabiting. If they knew the problems associated with it, they would probably avoid it. FSIAD occurring through cohabitation is probably unknown or at best poorly understood. Cohabitation involves couples living and sleeping together freely without marriage (LTWM). They usually create an arrangement in which the woman, if she has significant self-respect, or the fear of God, minimizes sexual intimacy. She may be a member of a church and an active church worker. If the man is also a Christian, the likelihood of the picture I am about to describe increases significantly.

The good girl knows deep down within her that she shouldn't just give herself sexually to the man that cheaply before marriage. So she limits canoodling and the ultimate act of intimacy to about once every three to four weeks. Since they both may have busy lives, nothing may happen for six to eight weeks while they focus on school or work. But unknown to both of them, they are gradually developing a pattern for their eventual sex life after marriage. Terrible isn't it! After they marry, several intimacy problems extending beyond sexual intimacy begin to emerge. My focus will be only on the sexual intimacy part and how that problem usually develops.

First, the woman's mind is gradually programmed to believing that the man is okay with sex once every eight weeks. With this new program running in her brain's computer, she now believes sex once every three or four weeks is quite generous! After she marries, she intends to keep things that way because she was programmed that way. Once every eight weeks is about 6 or 7 times a year. Moments of spontaneous sexual arousal in the woman might occur occasionally leading to SSEs, but these will be rare moments. Gradually, both man and woman become desensitized to their natural rhythms and sexual needs. The man has no right to complain because he has no real legitimate claims yet and he is sure things will change after they marry. Ironically the sexual area is where men hope women will change and women hope men won't change. With everything else, men hope women won't change and the women hope the men will change. Ironic.

A second thing also happens through the months or years of cohabiting that destroys intimacy after marriage. The woman becomes desensitized to the man's natural sexual needs. Whether twice a week or twice a month, the man's normal sexual needs will often times be more frequent than the number in the woman's head. Once a week for the man is still four times a month whereas the number in the woman's mind might be once every 6 weeks. In twelve weeks the man will be expecting 12 SSEs whereas the woman has been programmed by cohabitation to believe it is two in twelve weeks. That's a huge gap and the man is going to suffer. The wife has been programmed for a longer interval between SSE's and has become desensitized simultaneously. The man on the other hand is not desensitized to his own sexual needs. His sexual needs will remain unchanged after the marriage. He just wasn't complaining before the marriage because he had no rights. He is thinking, hoping or believing that his fiancée will change after they marry and meet his needs more frequently once he commits. He is unaware of how cohabitation is dangerously reprogramming her mind so that after she becomes his, their sexual rhythms will be distorted if not almost destroyed.

This distortion may be difficult to unravel and usually hides under conflicts of incompatibility. The sad part is that the woman's desensitization can be extremely difficult to change after they marry. And except she is threatened by divorce or other crisis, she is unlikely to budge or seek help.

Can this be fixed? Perhaps. The first and best way to deal with the distorted programming and desensitization is to avoid it in the first place. Do your possible best to wait till after marriage. My wife and I took a vow of purity and covenanted with God to help keep us pure. It isn't just how far you go but how often and how defiant you are about having sex before your marriage that sets the destructive programming and desensitization in place. To add spice to it and keep us on our toes, we put our lives on the line in the covenant. Eighteen years later, we are still as passionate about each other as when we first married. Too old-fashioned for you! Perhaps a peaceful and happy marriage is also too old-fashioned for you. Good luck then.

The second option is to go on pretending as if you're both married while you're not and be sexually active. If you do that, there'll be nothing much left to explore about each other by the time you finally marry each other. You have basically abused each other. Your passion if not your love for each other will fizzle quickly when conflicts arise. This creates another problem that puts the woman at a great disadvantage in the relationship. The man is likely to think the woman is cheap. He enjoys the canoodling but at the same time is more likely to cheat on her. She will be lucky if the man marries her and even if he does, he still won't value her like a like a queen in his castle. If he does, he is a rare one indeed. Don't forget also that the man may have been completely desensitized to the woman's emotional needs. In most instances, the man dumps her before they marry.

Another unanticipated blow from cohabiting occurs when the woman "gets religion". When a woman gets "religion", she may become convinced that the only way to be absolved of the guilt from all her past sexual sins is to give "penance". Once she realizes that cohabitation is a sin called fornication, she goes back in time to try and fix the past. Since she really cannot travel back in time, she figures out that the best way to cleanse herself of her premarital sexual sins is by practicing sexual abstinence in her marriage! To carry out this penance, she believes that each time she turns down her husband's sexual advances, she is cleansing herself. In her mind, the more she turns her husband down, the cleaner she thinks she is getting. Again, some women who did not cohabit but simply were not virgins when they married may also carry out this penance. The negative tension built up as the husband's physical needs are neglected or denied may lead to conflict and hostility. Penance may lead to the downfall of the marriage. Led by her guilt, the "religious" woman may be misguided that sex is a sin or a necessary evil even in marriage rather than a gift from God. She may lose interest in sexual intimacy and hope and pray her husband loses interest too! She may even pray and fast for her husband to lose his libido! Such a woman may eventually fit the criteria for and be diagnosed with FSIAD. You can be sure that no pill will cure this condition of guilt or ignorance from any woman's conscience. No real or deepening intimacy can occur in such a marriage and sex will eventually become a burden too difficult to bear. The marriage again may collapse or become unfulfilling.

If the cohabiting couple are uninhibited by any cultural, religious or psychological restraints, they may engage in continuous acts of sexual intimacy until they reach a saturation point. At this saturation point, they will need more stimulation to get aroused and maintain arousal. One or both of them may then start watching pornography. This will eventually lead to addiction. No longer able to satisfy each other's needs, they feel compelled to engage in sexual experimentation, share naked pictures of each other by text or online, engage in phone sex or different shades of sadomasochistic sexual behaviors along with addiction to pornography. This eventually leads to sexual desensitization. This may again lead to FSIAD in the woman. The man does not escape from his own share of sexual dysfunction, as you're about to discover in the next section.

Sexual Desensitization, MHSDD & Pornography

Pornography creates an excitement phase following which subsequent viewing of the same material fails to generate the same excitement. It therefore forces the individual to seek more and more intense erotic material to get the same level of thrill and dopamine rush. This can go on until the person is engulfed completely spirit, soul and body aka addiction. This escalating-type of addiction renders the addict paralyzed and socially inept. They no longer find their partner as attractive as before and their imagination and creativity shuts down almost completely. The women may develop FSIAD, the men pornography-induced erectile dysfunction, (PIED) or Male Hypoactive Sexual Desire Disorder, (MHSDD).

According to British researcher Gary Wilson, Internet pornography is destroying the sexual performance of young men. As the men watch pornography they get a thrill, their dopamine levels rise, and if they continue watching, physical changes start taking place in their brains. Most of these changes take place in the brain reward circuits. Dr. Nora Volkow, director of the National Institute of Drug Abuse (NIDA) and colleagues have demonstrated a decrease in dopamine D2 receptors in cocaine, heroin and alcohol addicts. There is a decrease in dopamine receptors as well as a decrease in dopamine transporters addicted to pornography. Young men in their twenties and hooked on Internet pornography are diagnosed with erectile dysfunction frequently enough to raise concerns about the problem. Most of these young men do not respond to Viagra because the problem is not down there in the genitals but up in the brain pleasure center. Perhaps flibanserin might work for these men too! These young otherwise healthy men with erectile dysfunction didn't get to this point by accident. They journeyed through a 3-

stage process to land in the jungle of pornography addiction. This 3-stage process was described by Gary Wilson in his TEDx talk and is the result of a weaker brain numbed by pornography. At the first stage, there is a reduced reaction to the pornography site by the addict. This forces the addict to seek more and more intense erotic material. Next comes the reduction in libido and finally erectile dysfunction. Could this be what happens in women addicted to or watching pornography also? Ran Gavrieli, a lecturer and former pornography addict has a TED talk posted on the Internet on October 26, 2013. He said Internet pornography conquers your mind and has both addictive and paralyzing properties. Cambridge University's Dr. Valerie Voon showed how the brain reward center called the ventral striatum lights up more than twice as bright in pornography addicts compared to non-addicts when both groups were exposed to the same pornographic material. When I looked at the functional MRI (fMRI) slices of her subjects, (on the internet, not in person), it looked more like five to eight times brighter in the addicts. I wonder if the fMRI can be used to identify individuals addicted to pornography but who deny they are addicted! Pornographic material causes the ventral striatum of pornography addicts to light up just as much as cocaine causes the ventral striatum of cocaine addicts to light up. When a woman engages in porn, the likelihood exists that similar brain changes will take place in her brain. Without intervention, the ability to function in a normal relationship maybe lost temporarily depending on whether or not the addict is willing to quit watching pornography. If a woman loses this ability to respond naturally, it is unlikely that she would want to be intimate with a man without intense therapy. Such therapy would require that she first admit she has a problem with sexual intimacy that may have stemmed from pornography, a confession most women are not willing to make. How rampant is pornography addiction in women? During an interview with talk show host Joni, former porn star Shelley Luben said 25 percent of women, one in every four women in the church, admit to watching pornography. For men in church, Shelley quoted 70 percent. When addiction sets in, nothing is ever enough. Remember the lady that divorced her husband because he refused to play one of the roles she wanted him to play from E. L. James' *Fifty Shades of Gray?* She is a high-powered British lady banker earning over $600,000 a year. A woman divorcing her husband for not doing the erotic things in a novel may be addicted to pornography. Her mind may have been reprogrammed to think her husband is just a sex object she can manipulate at will.

Sex is good not just for humans but for animals too. Researchers have shown that sex was associated with growth of brain cells in mice hippocampus according to a study done at Princeton University. Sex reduced anxiety in rats as well as the negative effects of the hormone cortisol on other systems of the body. People who report more sexual intercourse have lower blood pressure when performing arithmetic or speaking in front of a crowd. These tasks associated with high stress levels. In the Happiness Study reported in *The American Economic Review*, 900 women were asked how various daily activities made them feel. Intimate relations topped the charts. Another study by the *Bureau of Economic Research* found that increasing sexual intimacy from once a month to once a week led to happiness levels equivalent to getting a $50,000 raise! The type of sex mattered according to the study and those who cheated on their wives or paid for sex were less happy.

Not only is sex good for the body and the soul, an orgasm was also found to soothe the same part of the brain calmed by antidepressants. So an orgasm may reduce the incidence of depression. If that is true a woman simply needs to shut down many of the automatic negative thoughts (ANTS) that crowd her mind and simply enjoy herself with her husband when it's time for bed. She'll be healthier. Who knows what the power of the healing touch on the man's hands would do for her breasts in lowering her risk of breast cancer because he touches it with such gratitude and pleasure.

Sexual Desensitization Through Promiscuity
Sexual promiscuity can desensitize any man or woman to their natural sexual rhythms. Cohabitation, multiple sex partners are all risks we take that could distort or destroy our natural sexual rhythms when we finally marry.

Sexual Desensitization Through Perversions
Anyone engaged in any form of sexual perversion is probably desensitized to his or her natural sexual rhythms already. Pornography, polyarmory and

orgies are likely to lead to or be precursors of sexual desensitization. Sexual desensitization eventually prevents the development of the deepest possible connections between the spirit soul and body of couples in marriages. Anything that would lead to this deficiency should be avoided because marriages meant for the long haul are worth the sacrifice you have to make. Remember that after you marry, there should be enough to discover and keep you both excited for the rest of your lives.

Chapter 17

THE LIES WOMEN BELIEVE
That Hurt Their Marriages

Men believe two simple lies about sex in marriage. The first is that once they have their orgasm, everything will be fine in their marriage. The countering truth to that is that nothing will be fine until your wife has her own orgasm. Once she does however, things will be much finer than you can both imagine. The second lie men believe about sex in marriage is that their wives will always be there for them sexually. Most married men will disagree, as would most married women. There is a saying that what a man can do a woman can do better and so women believe more lies about sex in marriage than men. These are the lies I have encountered in addressing or researching marital problems.

THE LIES WOMEN BELIEVE

#1. Sex is the Forbidden Fruit Adam and Eve Ate in the Garden of Eden. The less I eat or enjoy, the better, the holier I get. Nothing can be farther from the truth. You don't get holier by avoiding sex in your marriage. You frustrate the gift and grace of God most of the time you maintain this paradigm.

#2. My Husband is Okay When I Don't Respond To His Sexual Advances.

No he is not okay. He is angry and building up some unnatural anger that can only be defused by tender intimate physical pleasure with you. If you don't find the time to be intimate with him, you may create a time bomb of rage. Or perhaps you already did.

#3. Enjoying Sex Means I am Filthy-minded.

Not if you're married. And even if you're not, that still doesn't mean you're filthy, it means you have a natural desire that better be put in its proper context before you get hurt emotionally or physically. Many women who are having problems sexually today have been directly or indirectly traumatized by wrong exposure to sex earlier in life. They refuse to admit this could be the problem because they enjoyed it at the time. But the conscience knows when and where sex is safest and best. Violating or ignoring that knowledge only allows guilt to reside deep within your soul. That guilt may then resurface as a desire for the infamous penance when you marry. So at a time when the woman should be enjoying sex with her husband freely, she seeks absolution from the sins of her past sexual encounters by refusing to have sex with her husband. God forgave her but she tortures herself with her own guilt.

#4. Enjoying Sex With My Husband Will Make Me Look Cheap

If you don't have sex, you will cheapen your marriage by subjecting it to unnecessary sexual tension or adultery. You may expose your husband to sexual temptation that he either struggles with or gives in to. Remember the man is linear and he doesn't need an emotionally perfect reason to have sex, he just needs to be aroused. God designed men this way so that women can effortlessly influence them, making sure that men can be sexually aroused anywhere anytime. It is probably God's greatest pet project for creation. Generating sexual arousal in men is the easiest thing we know about human behavior to date! He'll think you're cheaper if you don't engage him quickly enough in the bedroom after you marry. If you don't engage his advances positively, he may resort to pornography. This would make you even cheaper because he values a free and cheap cadaveric picture more than he values you for meeting his sexual pleasure.

#5. Never have an Orgasm. It Killed My Mom And it Could Kill You Too.

This may very well be true if you are seventy-five years old, have severe coronary artery disease, have had a coronary bypass or stents, have heart failure, high cholesterol, smoke two packs of cigarettes a day, have blackened toes that have been amputated and a major stroke. If you don't have any of these and are married, an orgasm will do you a lot of good than you can ever imagine!

#6. I Have a Headache, I Don't Need Sex

If it's true that you have a headache, an orgasm may be the best cure for your migraine. While writing my "Women and Weekend Migraine" article in the emergency room in 2005, I asked several of the nurses if they complained of headaches to their husband as an excuse. To my, surprise, most of them said yes. Even the kindest and most genuinely caring nurses said yes. I was shocked. A headache can be cured by an orgasm. Some studies have actually shown that men have more sex-related headaches than women but they still go ahead. Perhaps the pressure of having to perform creates the tension within! Dr. Couch, chairman of the department of neurology at the University of Oklahoma Health Sciences Center has a "Couch "treatment for migraine – an orgasm. He was recruiting migraine patients for a drug study when he met a 40-year old lady that worked for the state of Illinois as a mid-level manager who told Dr. Couch very bluntly,

> *"If I could just have a good, banging orgasm, it can stop my migraine cold. But my husband just divorced me. I don't need a pill; I just need a phone number."*

Migraine sufferers have greater sexual desire than non-sufferers according to Wake Forest University researcher Timothy Houle, PhD. He studied 37 women and 31 men reporting headaches. 90% were unmarried. 23 of them suffered migraines while 36 had tension headaches. Those with migraine had 20% more sexual desire than those without migraine. In the group, the men had 24% more sexual desire than the women. Female migraine sufferers therefore appeared to be like normal males without migraine in their sexual desire levels or libido. Stefan Evers, MD, headache specialist at University of Münster, Germany, surveyed a thousand patients using questionnaires to inquire about their experiences with sexual activity during headache attacks. 4 in 10 responded. 800 had migraine and 200 had cluster headaches. A third of them engaged in sexual activity during a migraine or cluster headache. Of the migraine suffers, 60% experienced relief while a third experienced worsening of the migraine with sex. The reason for the worsening may be that sex without orgasm may worsen the headache and an orgasm may fix that. Who knows! Psychiatrist Dr. Amen suggests:

> *"Rather than use migraine as an excuse not to have sex, use it as an excuse to have sex. Having an orgasm can alleviate or completely eliminate migraine."*

Sex related headaches are three times commoner in men than in women.

#7. My Husband Should Always Make the Move

After a while, he might get tired of making the first move. Notice how an affair often starts with a married man. The other woman finds something delightful in a married man and lets him know she likes him. He gets home and his wife totally ignores him or worse derides and nags him. He goes back out to the woman showering praises on him and showing appreciation. Let your husband know you like him and be genuinely honest about what it is you like about him. Make moves on him. Dress seductively. Visit Victoria Secret. Shower. Use deodorant and antiperspirants. Bring out your erotic self. God made you that way and wants you to show your husband and give him the best sex he can ever have. Why have your husband pay a prostitute to get what you were designed by God to give him as his wife? Beats me!

#9. My Husband Will Never Cheat on Me

It depends on how you define cheating. Hopefully, he is a God-fearing man who is not sex-starved by a religious hypocrite wife with no medical illness or contraindications to a good sexy romp. Do you sleep enough with your husband for him not to desire to cheat on you when he is faced with temptation? Why not

#10. Once I Turn 50 years, I Will Stop Having Sex

Your husband might agree if he is eighty years old, thirty years older than you! If he is not, be careful making such a statement. A very dear friend shared at a conference the plight of one of her good friends, a woman about to celebrate her 50th birthday. The woman started boasting to my friend that she was glad she was getting to 50 and will not have to have sex with her husband anymore. My friend, a TV show host, minister and physician, wisely asked the lady if she had ever talked this over with her husband. The woman said "No, but I'm sure he will be fine with it". "Then let's ask him when we get home", my friend requested. On arriving at her house, the woman, with my friend right beside her, asked her husband if he would be okay with no more sex after she turns fifty. There is something wrong with her thinking the man said using a few words in frustration. It doesn't matter how old you are, you can still enjoy a good romp every time you wish.

#11. My Husband Can Never Leave Me

These days, claiming to be a Christian doesn't necessarily imply that you have a high moral code, sensitivity, compassion or even godliness. EZ married a stunningly beautiful woman who worked as a respiratory therapist in a Northern California hospital. One day this woman approached me so open-heartedly and vulnerably, I was a little guarded. Apparently one of the staff at the hospital where she worked had given her a copy of my very first book, *The 36 Well Kept Secrets of Successful Marriages and Divorce.* When a woman that beautiful open-heartedly approaches you and you are happily married and faithful, you ought to be fully guarded and alert. I was.

Noticing my guard, she quickly said she meant no harm, had read my book and just wanted to ask me a few questions about her divorce. Wow, that's better I thought. Sure, what would you like to know, I responded. She described her ex-husband as a man who loved her and the children and still does. So why did you end up divorced then? I didn't know sex was important to men, she replied. More curious, I decided to probe deeper, knowing she wasn't being seductive. She said she is a Christian, had married a wonderful man and they had started having problems she attributed to the normal growth of the marriage. She immediately blurted out that she wasn't taught in church that sex was important to her husband or her marriage until she read my first book published back in 2001. As a result when they started having problems, she decided to go on a month of fasting with sexual abstinence of course. No sex and only one meal in

146

the evenings. Once she completed this fast, she decided since the problems had only worsened, to go on a 90-day fast. I interrupted her at this point to ask her how her husband felt about the 30-day fast. She said that her husband was unhappy about the total abstinence from sex for thirty days. "So you didn't both agree to the thirty-day fast?" I asked. No, she replied. "So how did you move to the ninety-day fast then?" Ladies and gentlemen, if your spouse doesn't agree with your 30-day fast, should you move to a 90-day fast, a total of 120 days? Only if you want your marriage to breakup! Well I thought that since we were having worsening problems that could not be resolved with a 30-day fast, a 90-day fast would be more effective. She said she didn't realize at the time that simple little things like having sex with your husband could save your marriage! I then asked how her husband felt about the ninety-day fast. He seemed quite upset, she responded. Then with a flushed face and this time with the pain more obvious as I observed this partially grieving woman seeking closure, she said her husband, now ex-husband, said if she was going on a 90-day fast, he too was going on a fast and "we'll see". They both went on the fast and midway through the 90-day fast, her husband packed his things and left, saying she wasn't ready to be a wife. The husband filed for divorce, yet remained a loving father to the children. She knew she lost a man who loved her and her children. I asked her why she thought her marriage ended and why she still thinks the man loves her after abandoning her. She said very bluntly that she had asked counsel from church members and that she never got any useful advise on how important sex was to the man she herself loved. So I asked the final question, if you have been available sexually, would the man have left? Her response was obvious. You figure it out!

#12 My Husband Didn't Marry Me for Sex.

O yes he did! He's just also interested in companionship also. A man gladly trades his freedom as a single man for sex and will accept all the responsibilities and liabilities that come with marrying. Take sex away from marriage and most men will never even consider an engagement. So it's an ambiguous question to ask your husband if he married you for sex. Of course he did. Be reasonable as a wife and just accept it. Your husband married so he could have sex with you. That's the number one reason and that doesn't make you cheap. He didn't marry so you guys could go shopping at the mall or listen to how your day went. You do those things with and for each other as the other benefits of companionship are expressed and spiced up through healthy sexual intimacy. For most men, no sex means, no marriage.

#13 We're Not Obligated To Meet Each Other's Sexual Needs.

Yes you are. The only people not obligated to meet each other's needs are boyfriend and girlfriend or fiancées. If you're married, within the context of your marriage, the husband or wife cannot have a surrogate sex partner. That leaves only you to meet each other's sexual needs.

#14. I Don't Feel Like It

Stop believing this. It has caused many marriages to breakup. The street term for FSIAD is frigidity and most women are not frigid. They just say they're not ready when they might be. Dr. Meredith Chivers showed that many a time that a woman is exposed to erotic stimuli, she becomes aroused. The women in her study however denied that they were aroused subjectively even though vaginal wetness and increased vaginal blood flow were recorded. These women were sufficiently aroused physically but reported that they were not as aroused even though measurements that could not lie revealed otherwise. Why women do that beats me. So perhaps the incidence of FSIAD may be much lower if women actually cooperated with their own bodies. Female sexuality is complex enough without this denial. The next time your husband starts fooling around with you, remember that you may be trying very hard to disconnect from the reality of your own sexuality for reasons that are not well defined by behavioral scientists to date. Also remember that if you continue this behavior and it becomes an ingrained habit that is difficult to break, you may lose your marriage or put it in jeopardy of infidelity.

#15. If I have Sex Regularly, My Beauty Will Fade

A thirty-three year old Santa Clara county employee said she had a "no-sex-after-8'oclock" rule in an article at www.marriagemissions.com. That same article quoted Al Cooper of the *San Jose Marital and Sexuality Centre* in San Jose, California, as saying that "In our society, it's more culturally acceptable for the woman to have no sex drive."

The 33-year old Santa Clara County employee eventually went through a divorce but whether this was finalized remains unknown. The advice this regretful woman gave was "find time to respond to your partner's advances". That's my parting advice to any mentally balanced married woman.

Failure to respond to your partner's advances can kill your marriage faster than you can imagine. I'm sick and tired of hearing about women who go for counseling after almost ruining their marriage through sexual starvation. Why did they even marry these men in the first place? If you're married, sleep with each other as much as you need to for as long as you're capable. It's pretty obvious with all the research done that women may deny that they are sexual beings and try to be sexually indifferent to their husbands for whatever reason. It is better not to marry than to marry if you don't feel sex is important. Otherwise you may end up diagnosed with a psychiatric condition such as FSIAD and then be put on a pill with dangerous side effects. Worse, you could have children, open the doors of infidelity and end up with a broken home, a sexually transmitted disease, divorce, unpaid alimony and child support while raising children without a positive male influence or father. If you enjoy sexual intimacy with your husband, you will feel more beautiful and have an unusually healthy glow about you. Only prostitutes age with intimacy because they are constantly trading their soul for money. Your beauty doesn't fade with frequent marital sex. It glows.

#16 The Woman's Needs are Far More Important Than The Man's.

I hear some preachers say this a lot. It's a lie of the devil! There is no healthy balance in any marriage that operates on this lie. The needs of both partners are important. Where is the equality feminists are fighting for in such a paradigm? Any balanced and healthy marriage allows the needs of both partners to be heard and met. Neither husband or wife or the children is more important. This paradigm is a dangerous one based on attempts to pacify women but it creates an imbalance that's unhealthy to the wellbeing of the husband and eventually the whole family.

In *What Every Woman Wants*, author Daniel Bergner narrates the plight of a husband whose wife said if only her husband helped more at home, she would be more intimate with him. The man scrubbed pots, cleaned dishes, dusted, painted, changed diapers and cooked, all to no avail. This man's plight can be seen in many households where the women fail to meet the man's sexual needs but blame their indifference on a dangling carrot of domestication. This behavior may be indicative of toxic ignorance or an undiagnosed and yet to be discovered psychiatric illness. The man who wanted to burn his house down because of sexual deprivation was also a gentle man: he cooked, scrubbed, cleaned, took care of the children and worked two jobs. Yet his wife would not sleep with him. That brings me to the topic of ...

Chapter 18

WHY WOMEN WITHHOLD SEX

Why do sexually captivating women married to good men regress after marriage into the role of the dispassionate sexually uninterested or inactive wife? In the absence of dyspareunia, why would a woman not want to sleep with a good husband who is there for her emotionally, mentally, financially, spiritually and physically? Dyspareunia, pain during intercourse, may be a factor. Other medical problems requiring a gynecologist's or primary care physician's evaluation may be responsible. Something can be done and should.

If a woman has a tumor in the cervix and has pain during intercourse, it would be the intercourse itself that would quickly alert her to the tumor's presence before it spreads and probably save her life. If she has a tumor but is one of those who naturally do not want to be intimate sexually with her husband for months, the tumor may reach a dangerously large size or spread before it is discovered. Similarly, a fungating breast mass may develop in a woman who does not perform breast self-examine and does not want her husband touching her breasts because it arouses her and she is uncomfortable with her erotic self. By the time she discovers there is something in her breasts, the lump may have become a large cancerous mass that has spread all over her body.

From my observation of couples, I have some thoughts on why women fizzle up after marriage and sheepishly wait till their marriage collapses before doing something about sex in the marriage. Just look around you and ask, "What would happen if a woman doesn't meet her husband's sexual needs in today's world"? Is he just going to stay celibate in his own marriage or is he going to find a way to meet his needs? Christian women often delude themselves into thinking the Christian man has no way out because he loves God. The Bible says that a wise woman builds her house but the foolish plucks it down with her own bare hands.

When a marriage goes south because the wife is unavailable sexually, a wise therapist will often bring out the issue and look for potential reasons caused by the man. As you probably know, we men are often the source when a marriage goes south sexually. If the man is not found to be guilty of anything worthy of sexual deprivation, the therapist may then recommend that the woman be more available. There is no way a sensible therapist will recommend that a wife continue to deprive her husband of sex. Nor will marriage therapy favor a woman complaining that she is always busy and therefore has no time for sex. Of necessity, a man who doesn't help his wife with household chores will need to help more often. Some therapists are finding out that wives claiming they can't be intimate because the men don't help with chores are making excuses with no basis. While women are using lack of domestic assistance from the man as an excuse for their sexual deprivation, many men still don't get "cookies" no matter how much they do for their wives. I know enough of such men, a few confessing to me they were hooked on porn as an alternative until we worked prayerfully so the men could be freed. Some of these men's wives remained audacious and arrogant when confronted about their ruthless insensitivity to the man's sexual needs. I call this a form of insanity and this may very well be the group of women who need the Pink pill and will benefit from it the most. I know one lady who wanted to get a job out of state just so she could avoid intimacy and pretend she was still married.

No matter how much the woman hides behind "busy", effective counseling will only do one thing; bring the woman to the place where she needs to sleep more frequently with her husband. If she wants to keep her marriage and be happy, she will follow the therapist's advise. So why does a woman need hours of counseling just to do that? Is this some form of mental illness for some women, particularly those who do not have any reasons to withhold sex in the marriage? Even intelligent accomplished educated and beautiful self-confident women engage in this behavior and still wonder why their husbands are behaving in a strange way towards them? I don't mind them abstaining but why should they be puzzled about the man's weird behavior towards them or others? Isn't their withholding sex from their husbands in the marriage itself weird? A sexually deprived husband's weird behavior is often related to his discovery that he is trapped and the woman has no intentions of meeting his own needs while he meets hers. And God help that man if he has money and the woman married him just so she could divorce him and take his money. Unfortunately, quite a number of pharmacists, physicians and healthcare practitioners have run into this problem.

WHY WOMEN WITHOLD....

So why do women withhold sex and prefer to suffer? Why do they suddenly become more sexually available after going through brief therapy? Why is it that good men suffer from their wife's negligence in the bedroom? Besides the possibilities created by medical conditions such as reduced libido from drugs or medical illness, most women in the representative sample in the Pink Pill study were healthy women. One of the subjects said she was fine from the neck down when it came to sexual intimacy but something was wrong from the neck up. They didn't have to be that way but many chose to. Kaplan & Sadock's *Synopsis of Psychiatry* states that a woman withholding sex in her marriage is engaged in a form of violence against her husband. Perhaps penance is a form of violence also. When a woman's marriage is about to collapse, it's amazing how quickly she readjusts to meet her husband's needs despite continuing to have a busy schedule. All of a sudden with therapy, she is no longer too busy to be intimate with her husband. Michelle Weiner-Davis, therapist and bestselling author of *Fire Your Shrink* said many couples, close to two-thirds, solve their marital problems the moment they make the appointment to see a marriage therapist before the appointment date. Why does a woman need any other person to tell her to sleep with her husband before she does so? I respect and honor a woman's intuition and believe that intuitively, many will solve their problems without a therapist if in fact the problem stems from withholding sex, before the man walks away. You won't believe how many such women still argue and refuse to do the right thing until the man simply walks away.

CHAPTER 19

GUILT-FREE PLEASURE

If a woman has a healthy emotional bond with her husband, why would she refuse to be intimate with him? Besides thinking and believing she can get away with it, with there are several reasons for this behavior. First is ignorance about her alluring sexuality, beauty and erotic nature. If she is aware of how thrilling a desire she stirs up in her husband and even other men, she might want to give him what he needs.

The second reason may be that the woman does not understand her own natural sexual needs. While men are easily aroused and quick to see they have needs, women have a more complex sexual arousal pattern and they may misinterpret the signals their body is telling them. They may even presume they have no sexual needs.

The third reason is that women may have those self-sabotaging automatic negative thoughts ANTs, described in Dr. Daniel G. Amen's book, *Unleash The Power of The Female Brain*. These ANTs result from excess activity in the part of the brain called the anterior cingulate cortex (ACC). In women, this part of the brain is far more active than in men.

When the ACC is overactive, women find it difficult to switch between mental tasks.

The fourth reason is that some women play out dangerous subliminal tapes that undermine their marriages. Sometimes buried in their subconscious mind is the idea that they do not deserve a good husband. Perhaps she had done some things in the past she is ashamed of. Or perhaps her father walked out on her abusive mother and she now thinks she doesn't deserve the good man she has now married. She is married and happy but wants to sabotage her marriage and chances of happiness.

The fifth reason is ignorance of the man's simple sexual needs and how easy it is to give the man what he needs so he can leave her alone or before he becomes desperate enough to cheat or get hooked on pornography. Most men are okay having just five minutes of access to a woman's body. If the man needs more than that from a woman, it's either he is sex-deprived and you know it but have decided to ignore it, he has an insatiable appetite, or that there is a deep emotional bond between him and his wife. If the latter is the case, it means you're blessed and you probably have a man who wants to satisfy you sexually. Go back to chapter two and rule #2 on sexual availability for men. Share that information with your husband.

Another reason why women withhold is because the man doesn't know the anatomy of his wife's erotic zones. Every husband must know where the clitoris is located. A woman must also be comfortable with her body in order to help the man find the clitoris and explore each other's erotic nature. The clitoris is that part of the female anatomy that provides the greatest sensual pleasure for women during intercourse. Stimulating it gently is more likely to lead the woman to orgasm. Except for those who have found their "G" spot, and know how to stimulate it, the clitoris is universally accepted as the part that is stimulated in women to give them orgasms and sexual satisfaction. Learn to use the clitoral stimulation method by having the woman on top. Some preachers think the woman on top is a sin or abomination. The Bible says the two shall be one flesh but it didn't say which one must be on top. If you're married there'll never be a better place for you to enjoy sex than with your spouse. Have the courage to learn about each other's bodies and be kind to one another. It's not a sin, burden, weight or obligation to feel sexy and be sexually generous in your marriage towards each other. It is not guilty pleasure but guilt-free pleasure when a husband and wife are intimate physically. Just do it. And you can do it without the Pink pill if you have no psychiatric problem.

The final reason why a woman refuses to be intimate may be simply selfishness. A busy woman may choose to be unavailable because she knows that in the little time she and her husband have before bedtime only the husband will be able to have an orgasm. It would take twenty to thirty minutes before the woman reaches the plateau and orgasm and the woman may not have that much time. Knowing this nightcap would meet the man's needs but not hers, she refuses. "If I don't have time to reach an orgasm, you can't have one, no matter how little time you need", the woman seems to say.

MAN TO WOMAN TALK

If you don't want to sleep with your husband, it's not normal. Get help, find out why and fix the problem. If you don't think you're a lesbian, fix the problem before he chooses an alternative to your body to pleasure himself. He might be thinking of doing so while you're reading this section of the book! Yes, it's that urgent. If you don't think it's important to get help, you don't know anything about marriage, men or your own body. He married you because he sees a piece of heaven in you and he wants it, and all of you. That's why men marry women. Frankly I don't know what you women see in us men but I am encouraged that my wife sees something in me. Even if she sees nothing, she's there for me. We bless each other every day and are thankful. But women, you have it all. Because we're drawn to you and you get to pick. Only the richest men get to pick any woman they want the way a woman can pick any man she wants.

In *Unleash The Power of The Female Brain* Dr. Daniel G. Amen says the secret to being a great lover is to know the brain tendencies of your partner and then match your behavior to fit his or her brain. He further suggests 12 things you can do to embed yourself in your partner's brain and I have listed six of them here:

1. Take your partner's breath away
2. Do something special on a regular basis
3. Engage in lots of eye-gazing
4. Learn what pleases your partner sexually
5. Teach your partner what you like
6. Boost lasting love with sexual novelty

YOUR MEMORY CAN DISTORT THE PRESENT

Stop using your memory of past negative events to create automatic negative thoughts (ANTs). Doing so may destroy present and future pleasure and happiness. Let go of the past and forgive those who have hurt you. That includes your spouse. If they betrayed your trust, it may have to be earned and rebuilt again, particularly if emotional, physical or financial infidelity and damage occurred. If it wasn't infidelity, then let it go without seeking a therapist and just do what you need to do and spend the money budgeted for the therapist on each other. A cruise, trip to Paris, mall or favorite restaurant and the movies would do just fine.

Sadly, too many couples have locked themselves down into horrible behaviors they know they need to change but can't because of ANTs. Their pride gets in the way of change. Rather than just swallow their pride, they want to hide under the therapist's recommendation as an excuse for doing the right thing. They are unaware that only unconventional therapists will tell the guilty spouse that he or she is wrong. Most couples can do the right thing for their marriage without therapy except those that are mentally deranged. If the latter is the case, psychiatric consultation should be obtained.

ON MALE Vs. FEMALE CHEATING

When a man cheats it's biological, when a woman cheats, it's psychological. Men have a one-way switch for sexuality that seems to be permanently turned on. All it takes is a little sexual stimulus to generate arousal and the man is ready only to regret afterwards if he cheated. Many Presidential candidates know this all too well. For women, arousal as you have seen is more complicated and involves several steps, most of which are firmly within the woman's conscious control. A woman can never go to bed without intentionally planning to do so. In other words, while a man can accidentally impregnate a woman, a woman cannot accidentally get pregnant for another man. She must want to cheat before she can cheat. Sexist? So be it!

SEX IS A MARRIAGE LIFELINE

A marriage may survive for years or decades held together only by one thing, great sex. Someone once asked a constantly fighting couple why they stayed married. The lady's response and the man's was that the sex was so good it was worth keeping their marriage just for that. I hope Flibanserin will deliver more than the clinical trials have shown so far. That's because sex is a marriage lifeline and many marriages are crumbling because of women saying no in the bedroom. Men are far more simple and predictable sexually and with any cues from their wives will be more cooperative. Starving a husband sexually rather than be seductive and exciting means the woman is putting her marriage and herself at risk. She is at greater risk of not getting any sexual satisfaction herself, becoming emotionally disconnected and unfulfilled and eventually depressed. Perhaps that's why the statistics for FSIAD and depression in women are both too high. When a woman is happy, the world is always a better place. At home, work or play happy women brighten the atmosphere. But if she is unhappy and unfulfilled, she will create more gloom than she is going through herself.

Chapter 20

G-SPOT AND TYPES OF FEMALE ORGASMS

The orgasm is the fireworks of sexual activity. Every married woman deserves it and every man must know how to get his wife to that climax. This requires knowledge, patience and skill as well as an openness and cooperation with each other.

Breaking The Clitoral Sound Barrier
Debate about female orgasms amongst the experts has focused on Sigmund Freud's claim that a woman can only have vaginal orgasms. Susan Lyndon, a feminist argued that Freud's idea reeked of a ploy to oppress women and make them feel they need men before they could have an orgasm. So when Shere Hite published her best-selling book *The Hite Report on Female Sexuality,* all discussion about the female orgasm went clitoral. Then came along Rutgers University neuroscientist Barry Komisaruk and Beverly Whipple, a nurse and best selling author of *The G-Spot and Other Discoveries About Human Sexuality.* They broke the clitoral sound barrier by describing the existence of the erotic G-spot, named after the German gynecologist, Dr. E. Grafenberg, one of the first few to describe the G-spot.

The G-spot has been sold to women as a place of great erotic pleasure present in the anterior wall of the vagina and capable of producing multiple orgasms. Anatomists however insist that the G-spot is sensationalism, fake, with no documented proof. Yale School of Medicine urologist, Dr. Amichai Kilchevsky even wants the phrase G-spot discontinued! Anatomists believe that female orgasm is tied to the clitoris and the clitoris alone. Professors Komisurak and Whipple, supporters of the G-spot, have reported orgasms in women with complete spinal cord section at the thoracic T10 level, far above the nerves controlling the bowel, bladder, vagina, uterus, anus and rectum. Perhaps the G-spot is a mind body connection unrelated to feminist or non-feminist ideologies or what we currently know about female anatomy. We all know where science remains rudimentary with respect to mind-body connections. Some say the G-spot can be reached if the woman is on top or penetrated from behind. Whatever the case, a husband and a wife should derive pleasure from knowing and pleasing each other sexually.

Let the husband render unto the wife due benevolence: and
likewise also the wife unto the husband
- I Corinthians 7:3

We are all aware of reports of mothers reporting orgasms while breastfeeding their babies, making it clear that not all orgasms have to be genital. So it really makes no difference whether or not the G-spot exists as long as our women can be satisfied and feel good about the pleasure of intimacy and passion with their husbands. Oxytocin is released during breastfeeding and when women have uterine contractions during labor. It is also released during orgasms in both men and women.

(Carmichael et al, 1987). So is dopamine, the pleasure chemical.

The real issue is that when a woman refuses her husband's sexual advances, does that make her abnormal and in need of a psychiatric diagnosis or a prescription? I don't think so. The majority of women who refuse but don't need to may do so because that's what they've been culturally conditioned to believe they should do. Even if she has no sound basis for refusing, but does so, that doesn't make her abnormal. By refusing, she however needs to be made aware that she is refusing a health benefit and also putting her marriage at risk of infidelity. She is also placing her husband at greater risk of addiction to pornography. Refusing the man's sexual advances doesn't mean that anything is wrong with you. How many such refusals in a week or a month are acceptable for married couples? How may denials make an abnormality? Hopefully we will have an answer by the time DSM-X is published.

What about men who don't help with domestic stuff around the home? Should a pill be developed for them too? It is quite clear that women detach themselves quite often when sexually aroused by claiming that they are not aroused even when all the scientific data prove otherwise. If a woman wants a pill with little efficacy and serious side effects to help increase arousal, she should at least know that the pill is more of a placebo. She may already be aroused and in denial. As far as I know, Sprout never did studies like those of Dr. Chivers to see if patients were truly suffering from sexual arousal disorder physiologically. Nor did Sprout use any objective physiological measurements to determine if the pink pill was able to improve arousal. All they used were questionnaires.

If the women refusing to engage in normal sexual activity with their husbands are just expressing an environmental or cultural phenomenon and are therefore normal, then we have turned normal women who need to be courted wooed and loved in a lavishing way into abnormal psychiatric patients inadvertently. In the words of Francis Allen, MD, psychiatrist and Chairman of DSM-IV, this is pure over-medicalization of normal. It means over 10 million women between the ages of 25 and 64 diagnosed with sexual dysfunction need a drug that works on their brain so they can say yes to healthy intimacy. Isn't that sexist? It means we are entering the era of the *Stepford Wives*! Healthy sexual intimacy in marriage ensures greater intimacy and stability in the home. It should not require a pill if there is no mental or physical illness.

Based on the relative lack of effectiveness of the pink pill, I would say most of the women who will respond to the pill are not sick in the first place and do not need the pill to begin with. Taking the pink pill may only put them at greater risk of physical injury from the associated side effects. It would be much safer for such women to fantasize about their next SSE. They can become more seductive and spontaneous, accept their erotic sexual self and simply allow themselves to enjoy the pleasure of physical intimacy. They should know that their migraine could be cured by an orgasm, just as Dr. Couch ordered. The likes of Intrinsa and Libigel, Lybridos and Lybridas and a host of others have failed the ultimate FDA test of effectiveness. Probably because of marketing by the pharmaceutical companies, many women have been boxed into believing that failure of these drugs means someone out there has failed them. It's the greatest hoax. Look within. Become comfortable with your erotic self. Seduce your man. He'll be awakened to loving you in ways you can never begin to imagine if only you tried. While this advise may not work for you, I guarantee you that there will be millions more who will take it, run with it and see their marriage and sex life turn around 180 degrees.

Female sexuality remains intriguing and complex, and for those trying to develop a drug for arousal, they would have to come up with something strong enough to be a date rape drug. Even when they do, they'll still realize during their clinical trials that the woman can say no whenever she wants.

THE ORGASM GAP
This is defined as the ratio between the number of orgasms men and women have. For every three orgasms men have, women have only one. Frankly, I don't think that's because women have something wrong with them, but because the men are so excited being with them. Does the gap need a pill? You decide.

In closing, according to Dr. Basson, most women in long-term relationships do not frequently think of sex or experience spontaneous hunger for sexual activity. They dangerously cool off for reasons best known to them after the honeymoon. Strangely, some women don't even realize they've iced, while others think it's the man's fault and the result of not helping with chores in the house or wooing them. Some simply make up excuses as they go. Sadly, counseling often reveals these excuses to be nothing but false fronts to the woman's complacency. That happens a lot when the woman has the benefits of a God-fearing caring husband who helps with the bills and the kids.

If the woman wants to keep her husband and be happy she needs to wake up before the ice is melted by infidelity. Having observed many couples over the years however, I'll say that even those men who do everything the woman needs in the home rarely get enough action. For men, the primary sexual drive and hunger that led them to the woman they married doesn't change much for decades after marriage. That's an advantage women need to put to really good use and not abuse.

SEX AND SPIRITUALITY

Sharing your body joyfully is a measure of true spirituality. If you are married and you can't freely and joyfully share your body with your spouse, something is wrong. Your inability to do so may be for reasons beyond your control. But if you can share yourself with your mate and refuse to do so, you cannot be spiritual. It means you don't have enough spirituality or the level of spiritual awareness required to function effectively in your marriage. Jesus so loved the world he gave himself. What does it really cost to give yourself to each other physically in your marriage? You will fall short in commanding spiritual authority as a child of God if you don't. You definitely do not have enough spirituality to see that you are hurting your partner and damaging yourself by not sharing yourself. You may love yourself but you do not love your partner. Someone once said that sleeping with your husband only when you get what you want means you have become a prostitute with only one customer. You have turned your husband into a beggar and diminished the dignity of your own marriage. You have the power to make the change in your own life. Every woman has unbelievable power to make her man and her world a better place through the middle ground called sex.

Love freely, laugh heartily, listen carefully, learn diligently and give joyfully of yourself to your spouse. Be naked and never afraid with your spouse because you can afford to be.

In the beginning of the marriage was the middle, and the middle was sex, and it was very good.

As for the pink pill, you have all you need to make a choice.

FURTHER READING

1. *Saving Normal.* Allen Frances, MD.
2. *Mating in Captivity: Unlocking Erotic Intelligence.* Esther Perel. HarperCollins, New York, NY.
3. *The Emperor's New Drugs.* David Kirsch, PhD. Random House, UK.
4. *Anatomy of an Epidemic: Magic Bullets, Psychiatric Drugs and The Rise of Mental Illness in America.* Robert Whitaker
5. *It's Mostly His Fault: For Women Who Are Fed Up and the Men Who Love Them.* Robert Mark Alter.
6. *Sexual Intimacy in Marriage*: William Cutrer, MD, Sandra Glahn.
7. *What Do Women Want? Adventures in the Science of Female Desire.* Daniel Bergner.
8. *Guide to Clinical Trials.* Bert Spilker
9. *Kaplan & Saddock's Synopsis of Psychiatry.* 11th edition.
10. *The Proper Care & Feeding of Husbands.* Dr. Laura Schlessinger.

Videos Revealing Truths About Flibanserin:

Video 1 https://youtu.be/ZCG3fl0Aa-k
Video 2 https://youtu.be/qUUms7YmFX4
Video 3 https://youtu.be/aU5MgiCLNXs

Other books by Caxton Opere, MD

1. *5 Love Handles: Dr. Caxton's Marriage DNA*
2. *Divorce Medicine: How Divorce and Toxic Relationships Affect Your Health*
3. *The 36 Well Kept Secrets of Successful Marriages & Divorces*
4. *1 Roommate: Dr. Caxton's 7 Proven Steps for Choosing Your Ideal Mate*
5. *#1 Rule: Compatibility*
6. *GSP: God's Success Program*
7. *How To Enter a New Year*
8. *The DNA of Highly Successful Marriages*

About The Author

Caxton Opere, MD is the world's leading expert on the medical complications of divorce, a pre-litigation medical defense consultant that analyzed the death of the 33-year old who died in a threesome to show why the defense should never have lost the case. He was awarded Tumblr's 2015 January 2015 *100 Hottest Picks for Non-Profit Startups* for his work on the *Divorce Medicine Project*. He is a board certified internist, artist, husband and father who enjoys simplifying complex scientific research and transferring it into street level knowledge. He is the President of Divorce Prevention Ministries and CEO of Koth Clinic Inc. His passion is in lowering divorce rates and building highly successful marriages, providing effective affordable efficient healthcare. Some of his popular speaker topics include

Sexual Intimacy In Christian Marriages
How Divorce Kills
How Divorce Kills Productivity
Divorce and Heart Disease
How Anger Affects Your Heart
Divorce and Stroke Risk
5-Minute Compatibility Tests

www.doctorcaxton.com

Appendix

ANTs. Automatic Negative Thoughts. Resulting from Anterior cingulate cortex over-activity.

AWS. Antidepressant Withdrawal Syndrome

BRUDAC. Bone Reproductive and Urologic Drugs Advisory Committee

CAXTON SYNDROME. Hostility directed at a spouse in order to avoid sexual intimacy.

DAWS. Dopamine Agonist Withdrawal Syndrome

DSaRM. Drug Safety and Risk Management Advisory Committee

IAD. Intimacy Avoidance Disorder.

ED. Erectile Dysfunction

EFFICACY. How well a treatment achieves the intended effect under ideal circumstances

EFFECTIVENESS. How well a treatment achieves its intended effect in the clinical setting, when a patient does not fully comply with treatment.

FINISH. Flu-like symptoms, Insomnia, Nausea, Imbalance, Sensory disturbances and Hyper-arousal following antidepressant cessation.

FPO. Female Premature Orgasm

FSFI. Female Sexual Function Index. 19-item questionnaire

FSDS-R. Female Sexual Distress Scale- Revised. 13-item questionnaire.

FSIAD. Female Sexual Interest/Arousal Disorder

HSDD. Hypoactive Sexual Desire Disorder

MHSDD. Male Hypoactive Sexual Desire Disorder

JAMA. Journal of the American Medical Association

PGAD . Persistent Genital Arousal Disorder

PIED. Pornography-induced erectile dysfunction.

www.ingramcontent.com/pod-product-compliance
Lightning Source LLC
Chambersburg PA
CBHW072008090426
42740CB00011B/2138